LIBERTY IN LOUISIANA

A Comedy

LIBERTY IN LOUISIANA

A Comedy

James Workman

Edited by
Bruce R. Magee and Stephen M. Payne

2024
UNIVERSITY OF LOUISIANA AT LAFAYETTE PRESS

http://ulpress.org
University of Louisiana at Lafayette Press
P.O. Box 43558
Lafayette, LA 70504-3558

front cover painting: *Hoisting American Colors, Louisiana Cession, 1803*
Thure de Thulstrup c. 1903

Printed in the United States

Library of Congress Cataloging-in-Publication Data
Names: Workman, James, -1832, author. | Magee, Bruce, editor. | Payne,
    Stephen, 1963- editor.
Title: Liberty in Louisiana : a comedy / James Workman ; edited by Bruce
    Magee and Stephen Payne.
Description: Lafayette, LA : University of Louisiana at Lafayette Press,
    2024.
Identifiers: LCCN 2023045739 | ISBN 9781959569091 (paperback)
Subjects: LCSH: Louisiana--Drama. | LCGFT: Drama.
Classification: LCC PS3364.W256 L53 2024 | DDC 812/.2--dc23/eng/20231013
LC record available at https://lccn.loc.gov/2023045739

"To my fiancée Rachel and my sons Jeffrey, Jonathan, and Kerr. Thanks for reminding me not to take myself too seriously."

—Bruce

"For my parents, Ozzie and Inez Payne, who never wrote my script, but helped me pen my own."

—Stephen

TABLE OF CONTENTS

Preface
A Startling Discovery

Sometimes discoveries are accidental, and occasionally, serendipitous. Such was the case when I unearthed *Liberty in Louisiana* by James Workman. I was in the Lincoln Parish Library in Ruston, Louisiana, searching for information on John Wilkes Booth's time in New Orleans in 1864. To that end, I was reading *The History of Southern Drama*, a relatively thin volume penned by Charles S. Watson and published in 1997. Only thirty-one pages into Watson's study, I found reference to *Liberty in Louisiana*, a comedy written and published by James Workman in 1804.

Commemorating the Louisiana Purchase of the previous year, the text satirically explores the notion of cultural/ideological clash, all as a comedy of manners and all as one of early Louisiana's few examples of Federalist literature. The drama pits characters of Franco-Spanish and Catholic Louisiana, a region still under a monarchy, against those of the early United States Republic, largely Protestant and northern European, a nation struggling to find its identity at the dawn of the nineteenth century.

Fascinated with the play's premise, I realized that the text must survive someplace. More searching produced a short article from the journal *Louisiana History*: "A Denunciation on the Stage of Spanish Rule: James Workman's *Liberty in Louisiana*," also by Charles S. Watson. As I pored over Watson's analysis, I realized that the play was likely extant, at least until 1970, when Watson published his essay (and likely until 1997, the date, recall, of Watson's book-length study). I suspected this to be the case because Watson did not simply paraphrase or summarize the text. Instead, he quoted parts of it verbatim. This meant that he had a print of it at hand. Maybe, I reasoned, I could find it too.

A Lincoln Parish librarian helped me search WorldCat, and in a short time we found the object of our quest. In fact, we located multiple copies of the text, all of them saved as e-books or as microforms.

Within a few weeks, I received the text, as well as another shock: It was the second edition, one from 1804 and apparently the only surviving version of the script. To complicate matters, it was a digitized form of a microfilmed document, i.e., a copy of a copy. When I glanced through the text, not surprisingly, I noticed multiple places where the quality of reproduction was badly degraded. That state of affairs meant Bruce, some student volunteers, and I would spend several years restoring the text to a readable form.

Still, we finally had a print of this landmark in Louisiana drama. And from my perspective, I learned not to disdain happy accidents, even if they caused more than a little inconvenience. In fact, I've since uncovered a few more of these unexpected, even startling, finds in the months since we resurrected *Liberty in Louisiana*. All these are plays from Louisiana's earliest American period. For the present, however, all of them must await their own turns on the stage.

—Stephen Payne

Introduction
THE FIRST PLAY ABOUT LOUISIANA

Liberty in Louisiana by James Workman is, as far as we can tell, the oldest play involving Louisiana. The oldest play actually written *in* Louisiana seems to be *La Fête du Petit Blé, ou L' Héroisme du Poucha-Houmma*, written by Paul Louis Le Blanc de Villeneufve in 1814.[1] Workman wrote *Liberty in Louisiana* some ten years earlier in 1804 to support the Louisiana Purchase, but he did so in Charleston, South Carolina. We have not found any evidence that Workman ever produced the play in New Orleans, but he did stage it in Charleston, Richmond, and Petersburg (Virginia), New York City, and Philadelphia in 1804 and in Savannah in 1805.[2]

In his "Advertisment" before the play, Workman states that his purpose in writing the play is to show Louisianans "the great principles of general and genuine liberty, and holding up despotism to alternate derision and abhorrence."[3] He is more specific about the advantages of the Louisiana Purchase for the citizens living there toward the end of the play, when the general breaks character and addresses the audience:

> The LIBERTY we cherish consists in the laws which secure to us the enjoyment of all our natural and justly acquired advantages, and in the guarantees provided by our government for the preservation and improvement of those laws as well as for their equitable

---

1. Paul Louis Le Blanc de Villeneufve, *La Fête du Petit-Blé, ou, l'Héroïsme de Poucha-Houmma, Tragédie en Cinq Actes* (Nouvelle-Orléans: Courrier de la Louisiane, 1814), i, Bibliothèque Tintamarre, http://french.centenary.edu/houmma/houmma-1.html.

2. Charles S. Watson, "A Denunciation on the State of Spanish Rule: James Workman's *Liberty in Louisiana*" *Louisiana History* 11, no. 3 (1970): 251, http://www.jstor.org/stable/4231133.

3. See p. 21.

1

administration—*Legislative power delegated by these whom the laws are to protect—Trial by those whose own interest justice.*[4]

The superiority of the rule of law in a republic over its misadministration under monarchy is a major theme of the play. Workman even dedicates the play to "THE *Honorable* CHANCELLOR MARSHALL," i.e., John Marshall, then Chief Justice of the Supreme Court.[5]

Given that the play has apparently never been staged in New Orleans, what would the play tell the actual audiences back East? Certainly, it would reinforce the belief that republican government was superior to monarchical rule, but it would also show that the inhabitants of Louisiana could be successfully brought into the Union. They would greet the United States as liberators (not the last time that argument has been used), welcome the freedom that the United States bestowed, and take up the role of citizenship. This civic definition of citizenship competes with the idea of the United States as properly being an ethno-state, with citizenship limited to white, Protestant, Anglo-Saxon men with property.

The Louisiana Purchase pitted these ideas of national identity against each other. It was controversial because it brought a large block of French-speaking Creole Catholics into the union. Could they be integrated into the Protestant, English-speaking United States?[6] Practically nobody in the political establishment of the United States was as sanguine about the possibility as Workman. W. C. C. Claiborne, Jefferson's choice for governor of the Territory of Orleans, which would become the state of Louisiana in 1812, was as skeptical about the inhabitants as he was enthusiastic about the land and resources.

> The country on the Mississippi is fertile, happily adapted to cultivation, its productions various and abundant, the people wealthy, and in the enjoyment of all the necessaries, and many of the luxuries of life. New-Orleans is a great, and growing City. The commerce of the Western Country concentrates at this place, and there appears to

4. See p. 120. Emphasis in original.

5. See p. 20. Emphasis in original.

6. Vernon Palmer, interview with Bruce R. Magee and Stephen M. Payne, *Louisiana Anthology Podcast*, podcast audio, September 4–11, 2020, http://louisianaanthology. blogspot.com/2020/09/381vernon-palmer-part-1.html, http://louisianaanthology. blogspot.com/2020/09/382-vernon-palmer-part-2.html.

me a moral certainty, that in ten years, it will rival Philadelphia or New-York. I believe the citizens of Louisiana are, generally speaking, honest; and that a decided majority of them are attached to the American Government. But they are uninformed, indolent, luxurious—in a word, illy fitted to be useful citizens of a Republic. Under the Spanish Government education was discouraged, and little respectability attached to science. Wealth alone gave respect and influence; and hence it has happened that ignorance and wealth so generally pervade this part of Louisiana. I have seen Sir, in this City, many youths to whom nature has been apparently liberal, but from the injustice and inattention of their parents, have no other accomplishments to recommend them but dancing with elegance and ease. The same observation will apply to the young females, with this additional remark, that they are among the most handsome women in America.

The promotion of education and general information in this Province, ought to be one of the first objects of the Government. I fear that if education be left entirely to the patronage of the inhabitants, it will continue to be neglected; for they are not sufficiently informed to appreciate it's value. There are some respectable characters in and near New-Orleans, who were educated in France, that have pretensions to science, but they are unacquainted with our language and Government, and I fear they will not become useful citizens for some time.[7]

Jefferson and Congress decided that a bit of time must pass before the inhabitants of the Territory were ready for self-government. They decided not to follow the model of the Northwest Ordinance, which allowed a territory with a population of at least 5,000 free adult men to elect an assembly and send a nonvoting delegate to Congress. Instead, they adopted more of a viceroy system. Claiborne was both the chief executive of the territory and

7. William C. C. Claiborne to Thomas Jefferson, 16 January 1804, in *The Papers of Thomas Jefferson*, vol. 42, *16 November 1803-10 March 1804*, ed. James P. McClure (Princeton: Princeton University Press, 2016), 286–88. Founders Online, National Archives, https://founders.archives.gov/documents/Jefferson/01-42-02-0253; Julien Vernet, *Strangers on their Native Soil: Opposition to United States Governance in Louisiana's Orleans Territory, 1803-1809* (Jackson: University Press of Mississippi, 2013), 31–33.

the commander-in-chief of the militia. He did share power with a legislative council of thirteen locals, but they were appointed by Jefferson rather than elected by the inhabitants. The locals were painfully aware that Louisiana had not so much been liberated as it had been traded among three colonial powers. And Claiborne's negative assessment did not remain a secret for long. According to the editor of *The Papers of James Madison*,

> In February 1804 two Boston Federalist newspapers printed a truncated version of Claiborne's 2 Jan. 1804 letter, based on notes taken when it was read in Congress, in which Claiborne described the court system he had initiated and was inaccurately quoted as saying that trial by jury "would at present be a great inconvenience and trouble" to the residents of Louisiana. "They could not be made acquainted with it in fifty years. The principles of an elective government they cannot comprehend. A representative system would only bewilder them."[8]

By April 14, the printed version of the letter had made the trip to New Orleans, and Claiborne was writing to Madison to assure him that the anger of the locals had died down. This was the New Orleans that Workman entered, and the political and social realities of the transition may have dissuaded him from trying to stage the play in New Orleans. First, only a few inhabitants knew English and would be able to understand the play. Second, the Americans had not liberated the colony and established a republic. At least the Spanish had respected the locals enough to learn French. The territory's new governor, Claiborne, could not even speak French, and he seemed to think it would take fifty years before Louisiana would be ready for the self-government that the citizens of the United States experienced. This was *not* the situation to stage a play celebrating the Louisiana Purchase, and there is no evidence that Workman ever tried to do so in the region.

8. William C. C. Claiborne to James Madison, 14 April 1804, in *The Papers of James Madison*, Secretary of State Series, vol. 7, *2 April-31 August 1804*, ed. David B. Mattern, J. C. A. Stagg, Ellen J. Barber, Anne Mandeville Colony, Angela Kreider, and Jeanne Kerr Cross (Charlottesville: University of Virginia Press, 2005), 47–48. Founders Online, National Archives, https://founders.archives.gov/documents/Madison/02-07-02-0057. Vernet, *Strangers*, 31–33.

BIOGRAPHY

Workman's interest in the transformation of the Louisiana legal system came naturally to him, given that he was a lawyer. Born in Cavan, Ireland, probably in the 1770s, he began studying law in England at the Middle Temple in 1789. Since Catholics were prohibited from studying law at the time, Workman was probably a Protestant. In the play, Workman depicts his Scottish picaro Sawny M'Gregor in a far more favorable light than his Irish partner, Phelim O'Flinn, a hint that Workman himself may have been of Scottish descent.[9]

Workman immigrated to the United States in 1799 and moved to Charleston, South Carolina, in late 1801 or early 1802. He published and produced the play in Charleston on April 4, 6, and May 21, 1804. He also took his oath of citizenship on May 21 and moved to New Orleans shortly thereafter. Once there, he advanced quickly in the legal and political system. He became the secretary to Governor Claiborne and also to the legislative council, where he helped align Louisiana's continental legal system with that of the United States.[10]

Permit me to remark also that I have a considerable share in forming the system of laws by which the territory is now governed; a system which, combining the excellencies of the Roman and the English— of the Castilian and the American codes, innovated boldly where personal liberty required a change, and preserved with scrupulous solicitude, in spite of the barbarous ignorance that opposed us, all your laws, customs and usages, not incompatible with the acts of congress or the principles of the federal constitution.[11]

9. James Workman to Thomas Jefferson, 15 November 1801, in *The Papers of Thomas Jefferson*, vol. 35, *1 August–30 November 1801*, ed. Barbara B. Oberg (Princeton: Princeton University Press, 2008) 669–71. Founders Online, National Archives, https://founders.archives.gov/documents/Jefferson/01-35-02-0511; Charles S. Watson, "A Denunciation on the Stage of Spanish Rule: James Workman's *Liberty in Louisiana* (1804)," *Louisiana History* 11 (1970): 246–47.

10. Workman to Thomas Jefferson, *The Papers of Thomas Jefferson*.

11. James Workman, "A Letter to the Respectable Citizens, Inhabitants of the County of Orleans," *Essays and Letters on Various Political Subjects*, 2nd ed. (New York: I. Riley, 1809), 112. Internet Archive, https://archive.org/details/essayslettersonv00work.

On May 1, 1805, Claiborne appointed Workman to be a judge.[12] After that, things get murky. Workman got caught up in the Burr controversy during the winter of 1806–1807. His precise role in the events is the subject of considerable heated debate, along with everything else involved in the Burr's alleged treason. Untangling the details of those events lies beyond the scope of this introduction, but a basic outline of Workman's involvement reflects some of the values he espoused in his play. Workman was never charged with participation in the original conspiracy. Rather, he came into conflict with Governor Claiborne and General Wilkinson during the panic in New Orleans that arose when they heard that Burr was headed downriver with a militia. Wilkinson declared martial law and tried to suspend *habeas corpus*.[13] Workman's argument was that he tried to preserve the rule of law when he sought to grant writs to James Alexander and Peter Ogden, who had been arrested by Wilkinson late in 1806. In retaliation, Workman was pushed out of his judgeship, put on trial, and disbarred.[14] As happened with so many of the Burr conspiracy trials, Workman was found not guilty, and he argued that this amounted to complete vindication, both for himself, for the legal profession, and for the rule of law:

> A lawyer, the ornament of his profession and of his country, stepped forth for their protection; a man whose intrepid and high minded integrity stood far aloof from the degeneracy of the day, and defied the outrages of usurping power, the malice of dastard enmity, and, more hateful than these, the poisoned shafts of slander. In line, the accused were acquitted by a jury of their country; whose verdict evidenced

12.   Clarence Edwin Carter, ed. *Territorial Papers of the United States: Vol 9: The Territory of Orleans 1803–1812.* (Washington: Government Printing Office, 1940), 598. HathiTrust, https://babel.hathitrust.org/cgi/pt?id=osu.32435023718281&view=1up&seq=614.

13.   Ironically, the embodiment of disinterested justice in Workman's play is the American general who appears to establish order and bring a happy ending. The actual general who was at the ceremony transferring Louisiana to the United States was the same Wilkinson who declared martial law and secretly worked as a Spanish agent.

14.   *A Faithful Picture of the Political Situation of New Orleans at the Close of the Last and the Beginning of the Present Year, 1807.* Boston: Re-printed from the New-Orleans edition. Joseph Meredith Toner Collection, Library of Congress, https://www.loc.gov/item/01010864/; James Lewis, *The Burr Conspiracy* (Princeton: Princeton University Press, 2018), 220, 238.

their own courage as well as the innocence of those whom they had in charge.[15]

Another theme from the play paralleled in real life was Workman's opposition to Spanish rule in the Americas. The political thesis of the play is that republican liberty, clearly the superior form of governance, will replace archaic Spanish monarchy. When Workman got to New Orleans, he became active in the Mexican Association. While a title like that might indicate an organization that celebrates civic and cultural pride today, the organization of Workman's day was dedicated to organizing a military expedition against Mexico and Florida to overthrow Spanish rule. Workman never denied being a member of the association or that the association wanted to overthrow Spanish rule. Such plots abounded in New Orleans in the nineteenth century and eventually wrested Texas from Spanish rule. But there was no evidence that Workman's role went beyond talking, and the jury found him not guilty.[16] In his book *The Burr Consiracy*, James Lewis concludes that the charges about the Mexican Association were a pretext and that the real reason for his arrest was his welcoming of Kentucky militia general John Adair to New Orleans, with Wilkinson arresting Adair at the same time.[17] Workman left New Orleans but returned ten years later in 1817 and remained until his death in 1832 as a well-respected citizen of the town.[18]

PUBLICATIONS

At the beginning of *Liberty in Louisiana*, Workman reveals that he initially considered writing a pamphlet celebrating the Louisiana Purchase. He was certainly more comfortable writing political essays than plays. He only wrote this one play, but he published several letters and essays throughout his career. His first book, *Political Essays, Relative to the War of the French Revolution,* was published in Virginia in 1801. In 1809, he published a second collection, *Essays and Letters on Various Political Subjects*. It includes two letters he wrote against the British conflict with France in 1795 ("An Argument against Continuing the War for the Subversion of the French Government")

---

15. Workman, "Letter," 118.

16. Workman, "Letter," 148. Watson, "Denunciation," 248.

17. Lewis, *Burr*, 220.

18. Watson, "Denunciation," 249.

and 1797 ("A Letter to the Duke of Portland Being an Answer to the Two Letters of the Right Honorable Edmund Burke, against Treating for Peace with the French Republic"). He includes his version of events regarding the Aaron Burr controversy in New Orleans in "A Letter to the Respectable Citizens, Inhabitants of the County of Orleans together with Several Letters to Governor Claiborne, and Other Documents Relative to the Extraordinary Measures lately Pursued in This Territory" and "Copies and Abstracts of Certain Letters and Official Documents." He also includes his letter opposing the liberalization of divorce laws in Louisiana, "To the Legislative Council of The Territory of Orleans."

Workman's "Proposals for Publishing a Digest of the Laws of Castile and the Spanish Indies, with the Institutes of the Roman Code on which Those Laws Are Founded" addresses the persistence of the Castilian (Spanish) Code in civil law after the Louisiana Purchase. Spanish law books were generally unavailable in Louisiana, and, worse, the ones they had were in Spanish. So, as long as the Spanish law continued in effect, it should be available in a concise English version. Eventually the civil portion of the Castilian Code would be replaced in Louisiana by its relative, the *Code Napoléon*, both being derived from the Justinian Code, which first organized Roman Law.[19] One big difference between the *Code Napoléon* and Spanish law is that Spanish law was sprawling, disorganized, and had been accreted over centuries. Which laws were actually in effect was difficult to determine. Much of the vocabulary was medieval, as was the reputation of the Spanish legal system itself. The *Code Napoléon*, by contrast, was shiny and new. It had a systematic organization and embodied the values of the Enlightenment. It was seen as the most progressive legal code in the world.[20]

THE PLAY

The play itself is straightforward enough. Except for the songs, it is written in prose. Workman puts himself in the comedic tradition of Terence, Plautus, Shakespeare, and Molière, though freely confessing that he cannot claim to be on their level. To make his comedy fit his models, he cut the length

19. Vernon Valentine Palmer, "Sounding the Retreat: The Exit of Spanish Law in Early Louisiana 1805-1808." *Tulane European and Civil Law Forum* 31–32 (2017): 147, https://journals.tulane.edu/teclf/article/view/1581/1398.

20. Palmer, interview.

in half and divided his original three acts into five.[21] *Liberty in Louisiana* is a comedy of manners, as we would expect of a play influenced by these four playwrights. Accordingly, he fills his play with stock characters whom he uses to critique the shortcomings of the Spanish regime in Louisiana.

Furthermore, *Liberty* is the rare example of a Federalist play. Most Federalist material was directly political in nature, though there were examples of more literary efforts. Washington Irving, for example, is considered to have had Federalist tendencies.[22] Both Irving's "Rip Van Winkle" and Workman's play have characters who go to sleep as subjects of a king and wake up as citizens of a republic.

Driving much of the action of the play are the two picaros, or loveable rogues, the Irish Phelim O'Flinn and the Scottish Sawny M'Gregor. Anybody who remembers the duke and the dauphin from *Huck Finn* will recognize the type. Phelim and Sawny show up in New Orleans for the cession of Louisiana from Spain to France to the United States, which he collapses into one day for the sake of brevity. Of the two men, Phelim is much more of a rogue than Sawny, who has a more developed conscience. When he learns about Laura, the rich heiress with a $100,000 fortune, Phelim comes up with a scheme to pretend to be her admirer, the American Captain O'Brien, whom she has only met briefly. Since both Phelim and the captain are originally from Ireland and resemble each other, Phelim hopes he can fool Laura into marrying him before the American forces arrive. On the other hand, Laura, the maid Theresa, and Lucy Margland (the pregnant girl who followed Phelim from Tennessee after he seduced and abandoned her) conspire to marry Phelim off to Lucy to make an honest woman of her.

The Spanish judge, Don Bertoldo de la Plata, is the primary villain of the play, using his position to extort the maximum amount of bribes and other corruption before he loses his position with the arrival of the Americans. He embodies all that is wrong with the Spanish system. In addition to being a corrupt judge, he is also a *senex amans*, the stock figure of the old lover. He is tired of his wife and wants to run away with his ward Laura, along with her large fortune. His wife, Señora de la Plata, is equally tired of him and has her eyes on Captain O'Brien for herself. The interaction of all the secrets, schemes, and plots swirling through the play creates a lot of confusion and drives the action of the play.

---

21. See pp. 21–22.

22. Lewis Leary, "Washington Irving," in *Six Classic American Writers: An Introduction*, ed. Sherman Paul, 73–79 (Minneapolis: University of Minnesota Press, 1970).

In addition to the familiar stock characters, Workman may well have invented a new kind of stock character, America's form of the *deus ex machina*, which is the American army's cavalry riding to the rescue in the nick of time. In this case, it is not specifically the cavalry arriving, but it *is* the US army coming in to take possession of Louisiana and apply their more honest and enlightened legal system to the situation. They restore order to all the confusion and bring liberty to Louisiana.

Workman found it necessary to use stock characters in the play in part because he had never been to Louisiana and had limited information about it. Louisiana was already a complex society, little of which is reflected in the play. Absent are Indigenous peoples, Germans, and other groups that were in New Orleans at the time. It has no slavery, no African people at all. Even Theresa the maid is a free white woman, not an enslaved person. The world of *Liberty in Louisiana* has much more to do with the tradition of comedy Workman mentions than it does with actual events in Louisiana.

Workman works his opinion of the Spanish legal system into the play; in fact, one of the primary purposes of the play is to demonstrate the shortcomings of the Spanish legal system and the superiority of the American system, as he states in his "Advertisment" before the play. Charles S. Watson wrote the one important article on the play about just that: "A Denunciation on the Stage of Spanish Rule: James Workman's *Liberty in Louisiana* (1804)."[23] Expert on early Louisiana law Vernon V. Palmer divides Spanish law into various categories—including criminal, ecclesiastical, civil, and slave law—each with its own reputation in other European countries, especially Great Britain and France.

Vying for the most despised and feared areas of Spanish law were criminal and ecclesiastical law. In the arena of criminal law, Spain still used torture to extract testimony from people, as well as for punishment. Evidence was gathered behind closed doors, defendants could not confront their accusers, nor was there a jury to pass judgement. Even worse, defendants could be kept in jail for indefinite periods of time without a clear understanding of the charges against them. The reported situation in Louisiana after the Purchase fits this stereotype; Governor Claiborne sent the following report to Secretary of State James Madison:

> In the different prisons of this City I have found upwards of one hundred prisoners, some of whom had been there from ten to thirteen

---

23. Watson, "Denunciation," 245–58.

years, on Suspicions of crimes of which it does not appear they were ever convicted; and Some for offences of a very trivial nature. . . . Of the prisoners who have fallen within my province I have already released five, and shall proceed to set I believe the whole at large. Their detention would be attended with a heavy public expense, and would answer no good purpose, as it appears to me very questionable, whether any principle of Law would justify our noticing offences of which we had no cognizance at the time of their commission.[24]

The second category of Spanish law that earned particular horror and revulsion in Great Britain and France was ecclesiastical law, illustrated chiefly through the Spanish Inquisition. Extending from 1478 to 1834, the Inquisition loomed large in the imagination of English-speakers ever since rumors swirled that the Spanish Armada sought to bring it to England in 1588.[25] The Inquisition made its way to New Orleans with the arrival of Antonio de Sedella, better known as Père Antoine, and made its departure when Governor Miró deported him. Miró wrote about learning the Capuchin monk was mandated to start the Inquisition, "Al leer oficio de dicho Capuchino me estremecí" ("Reading the Office of the said Capuchin, I shuddered"). Père Antoine returned to New Orleans with the understanding that he would *not* be setting up the Inquisition there. But he continued to send reports of his investigations back to Spain until 1806, three years after the Louisiana Purchase.[26] While he took no action against people while they were in Louisiana, those who went to other parts of the Spanish Empire could have faced repercussions.[27]

Las Siete Partidas, Spanish civil law, based in Roman law, enjoyed a better reputation globally. Even Workman himself praised it, "The laws of Spain are generally excellent in themselves; for they are founded on the Roman Code,

---

24. Dunbar Rowland, ed., *Official Letter Books of W. C. C. Claiborne, 1801–1816*, 6 vols. (Jackson, Mississippi: State Department of Archives and History, 1917), 325–26. Internet Archive, https://archive.org/details/officialletterbo01claiiala.

25. Robert E. Scully, "'In the Confident Hope of a Miracle': The Spanish Armada and Religious Mentalities in the Late Sixteenth Century," *The Catholic Historical Review* 89, no. 4 (October 2003): 644, https://www.jstor.org/stable/25026461.

26. Nicole Biguenet Pedersen, "NOLA History: The Night the Inquisition Came to Town," GoNOLA.com, September 21, 2011, https://gonola.com/things-to-do-in-new-orleans/arts-culture/nola-history-the-night-the-inquisition-came-to-town.

27. Palmer, interview.

one of the most perfect and elegant systems of jurisprudence ever promulgated to the world." Nevertheless, Spanish civil law had three problems. First, it was vast and disorganized, having gradually built up over centuries. Second, many of the law books were rare and hard to find in the New World. Third, the procedures of civil law were expensive, convoluted, arbitrary, unreasonable, and slow. [28]

Despite the existence of a discrete code for the treatment of enslaved people in Spain, the *Código Negro Carolino* of 1784, Workman's promise of liberty for Louisiana did not extend to the enslaved there. In fact, the lot of those under this forced labor system grew much worse when the colony moved from the Spanish to the American legal system. Spain guaranteed enslaved people Sunday as a day of rest to observe the Catholic Sabbath. Additionally, they could grow small amounts of crops for sale or perform other work for hire and keep the money they earned, while in the American system everything belonged to the slaveholder. Furthermore, Spain granted those enslaved under its jurisdiction the right of *coartación*, wherein a person could pay for his or her manumission. If the slaveholder refused to sell the his or her freedom for a fair price, the enslaved person had standing to sue in court, which was not true in the American system, as the infamous *Dred Scott* decision established. Thus, the Spanish system provided the means and the opportunity for those enslaved to achieve freedom, which the United States did not. [29]

Because enslaved people do not appear in the world of *Liberty in Louisiana*, slave law is not an issue in the play. Civil law takes up the bulk of the hearings in the text: two of the cases Don Bertholdo hears involve inheritance issues, and he decides them on the basis of bribes. In one case, he takes half of the land that a widow had been left by her husband. In another, he takes a $1,000 bribe from one litigant to match the $1,000 bribe he had previously taken from the other, then splits the disputed property evenly between them. Mr. Fairtrade, a New England trader and reputed smuggler, bribes Don Bertholdo to look the other way rather than inspect his ship too closely. Bertholdo rejects butter, cheese, and copper coins as bribes, insisting on gold. But the cheap Yankee trader passes off coins that are merely cased in gold.

Another case involves both the Inquisition and civil law. Don Rodriguez appears before Don Bertholdo to complain about his case. He was held in jail on suspicion of doubting the pope's authority to pardon a murderer and then

---

28. Palmer, "Sounding the Retreat," 124.

29. Palmer, interview.

kept in prison for ten more years because he complained about being held for three years without a trial. Now that he is free, he wants his land back, but Don Bertholdo refuses.

Charles Watson argues that Don Bertholdo's character could have been modeled on an actual member of the Spanish government in Louisiana, Don María Nicolás Vidal Chavez Echavarri de Madrigal y Valdez. He quotes a letter by the French Prefect Laussat, who managed the handover, which called Vidal, "a cunning old dog who sells almost publicly his decisions, and who is the sole authority to pass judgment over the most important civil and criminal cases."[30] Pierre-Louis Berquin-Duvallon, a refugee from the 1793 slave revolt in Haiti, sought safety in Louisiana only to have the Spanish government confiscate his slaves, lest they spread revolutionary ideas to enslaved people in the colony. Berquin-Duvallon's anger with the Spanish civil court is clear in his attack on Vidal as being both corrupt and lecherous:

> For him everything is venal, and conscience and honor are meaningless words to him. How many acts of injustice and rapacity are not attributed to him? From how many unfortunate families has he not weakened the resources and drained the substance? A man as vicious as the unjust magistrate, in the very face of his countrymen, who are scandalised by his manner of living, and in a position where he ought to give others the example of good morals, is not that old rake with a monkey face (as ugly as it is impudent and evil), and wallowing in his celibacy, seen openly with a French mulattress, whom he has enriched with a part of his plunder?[31]

While corruption and inefficiency doubtless existed under Spanish rule, most historians consider the Spanish period in Louisiana to be rather well governed and not a great deal more corrupt than the French, Americans, or, later, the Confederates who governed the area. After the Spanish put down an early revolt, the locals accepted Spanish rule. Most of the regional judges during the period were not Spanish; they were locals who had enough money to pay for the positions.[32] (For example, the Spanish appointed the English-speaking American Daniel Boone to be a judge in the area of the colony that is now Missouri.) They hoped having an illustrious American as part of the

30. Watson, "A Denunciation," 256.

31. Robertson, *Louisiana*, 207–208.

32. Palmer, interview.

administration would encourage other Americans to come to the sparsely settled region. Boone selected a "judgment tree" to sit under while he heard cases, which he adjudicated according to his own common sense rather than any knowledge of Spanish law.[33] The same thing likely held true for the local judges in New Orleans.

Regardless of the actual state of the Spanish legal system in Louisiana in 1803, Workman likely would not have had much direct knowledge of it. So where did he get his notions of Spanish law? Vernon Palmer begins his article on the transition from Spanish to American law with a quote from Daniel J. Weber that nicely summarizes the stereotypes circulating about the Spanish government:

> From their English forebears and other non-Spanish Europeans, Anglo Americans had inherited the view that Spaniards were unusually cruel, avaricious, treacherous, fanatical, superstitious, cowardly, corrupt, decadent, indolent, and authoritarian—unique complex of pejoratives that historians from Spain came to call the Black Legend, *la leyenda negra*.[34]

Workman's attitude toward Spanish rule and Spanish law could have been formed from exposure to these stereotypes alone without any real acquaintance with the situation in Louisiana. Regardless, Workman was convinced the day of monarchy was done and that liberty had arrived for Louisiana, despite the efforts of those who sought to forestall it.

CONCLUSION

Liberty in Louisiana would be well worth reading even if it were only an example of a comedy of manners at the dawn of the nineteenth century. Quite apart from its political context, the play stands on its own for its sometimes-bawdy humor and its convoluted plot. Plus, it marks a critical point in the development of American frontier humor. Mark Twain's duke and dauphin may perfect the Mississippi River rascal of American Southwest

---

33. Mary Barile, interview with Bruce R. Magee and Stephen Payne, *Louisiana Anthology Podcast*, podcast audio, October 9–16, 2020. http://louisianaanthology.blog-spot.com/2020/10/386-mary-barile-part-1.html, http://louisianaanthology.blogspot.com/2020/10/387-mary-barile-part-2.html.

34. David J. Weber, *The Spanish Frontier in North America* (New Haven, CT: Yale University Press, 1994), 244.

frontier humor, but they exist in a legacy that starts with Phelim and Sawny. Workman also creates the trope of the American military showing up in the nick of time to rescue those in peril and restore order.

Yet the play's social and political context makes it uniquely important. We believe that it is the first extant play written about Louisiana, and it makes the argument that Louisiana would benefit from its inclusion in the United States, implying also that the United States would benefit by expanding westward. Despite being an immigrant himself, Workman taps into the American psyche when he portrays the intervention of the United States into foreign territories as a liberation, a rescue of the local inhabitants, even when they have no such opinion about the American interlopers. As both a study in the history of American drama and the history of Louisiana in popular culture, *Liberty in Louisiana* is a critical work ripe for additional examination and analysis.

ACKNOWLEDGMENTS

We want thank our editor, Devon E. Lord, for patiently guiding us through the publication process. We thank the staff at the Lincoln Parish Library for helping us acquire a scan of the 1804 edition of *Liberty in Louisiana*. Without that copy, the project would have never gotten off the ground. We also thank scholars Mary Barile, Vernon Palmer, and Julien Vernet for discussing their research into the era of the Louisiana Purchase with us to help us better understand the context of the play. Finally, we wish to thank all the students who helped with the proofreading of the microfilm copy—Thomas Barron, Patrick Bias, Alexis Byars, Caroline Cone, Rachel Cox, Jacob Desadier, Alexander Gaston, Chris Givens, Jason Gray, Natalie Hogan, Olivia Holmes, Sarah Howell, Jermesha Johnson, Lucky Lunalilo, Madeline Middleton, Madison Mitchell, Haley Sangali, Marc Schwartz, Julia Simpson, Jeffrey Tyler, and Morgan Wheeler.

Liberty in Louisiana

A Comedy

Performed at the Charleston Theatre

By James Workman

The Second Edition,
With Additions and Corrections.

Charleston,
Printed by Query and Evans, Broad-Street.
1804

South-Carolina District, to wit:

Be it remembered, that on the second day of April, in the twenty-eighth year of the independence of the United States,[1] James Workman, of the said district, hath deposited in this office the title of a book, the right whereof he claims as author, in the words following, to wit—"Liberty in Louisiana; a comedy," in conformity to the act of the Congress of the United States, entitled "An Act for the encouragement of learning, by securing the copies of maps, charts and books, to the authors and proprietors of such copies, during the times therein mentioned."

THOMAS HALL,
Clerk of South-Carolina District.

---

1. April 2, 1804.

TO THE

Honorable CHANCELLOR MARSHALL.

MY DEAR SIR,

PERMIT me to inscribe to you the following production, as a just though humble tribute to your well known talents, intelligence and liberality of sentiment, and in testimony of the grateful feelings inspired by the kindness and favorable regard which you have been pleased to shew towards Your most faithful,

and most obliged,

friend and servant,

THE AUTHOR.

ADVERTISEMENT.

THE production of a new play is an occurrence so rare in this part of America, that it may be requisite to explain why the following one was undertaken. It originated then in a desire, conceived early in the present year, to celebrate, by some literary performance, the cession of Louisiana to the United States,[2] and to display to its inhabitants the advantages they would derive from that happy event, by illustrating the great principles of general and genuine liberty, and holding up despotism to alternate derision and abhorrence. To attain these objects, the author at first designed to have recourse to the usual means of a printed pamphlet; but on considering the superior effect produced by sentiments embodied in natural character, and exhibited in some interesting story with the splendor of theatrical decoration, to delight the eye, or addressed occasionally to the ear as well as the mind, in strains of melodious music, he determined to make a dramatic representation the engine of enforcing his political opinions. With this view he framed a plot, which he did not suppose would have extended beyond two acts.... He had not yet entertained the idea of forming a regular comedy; a species of composition which the best critics leave classed among the highest pretensions in literature, and one in which none have ever excelled, but those endowed by nature with extraordinary genius, or those who have gradually risen to perfection by repeated trials, or by attentive consideration and accurate observance of dramatic effect. This was a kind of knowledge he had never attempted to acquire; it was even uncongenial with the nature of his principal studies, which had been directed to political philosophy and jurisprudence, he had not indeed neglected, in the course of a classical education, to peruse the works of Terence and Plautus, nor those which are in every one's hands and by every one admired, of Shakespeare and Moliere;[3] but so little did he possess of practical, *play-wright* dramatic information, that when the three acts, in which arrangement he at first composed the piece, were

2. The cession of Louisiana is the Louisiana Purchase. The ceremony for the handover to the United States occurred on December 20, 1803.

3. Shakespeare (1564–1616) is of course the most famous English playwright; Plautus (c. 250–184 BCE) and Terence (190–159) were Roman playwrights; and Molière (1622–1674) was French.

22

written in parts for the theatre, they were found to be of nearly double the length of any ordinary comedy. The play was then cut down, (slowly and reluctantly, as all who are acquainted with the prejudices and feelings of an author will readily suppose) to the size in which it appeared in print; again greatly diminished for the first representation, and afterwards still farther shortened to the form in which, on the second night's performance, it was received with general and reiterated laughter and applause.

It is doubtles improper in most cases for a writer to speak of his own productions. On the present occasion, however, an exception may be allowed in favor of one who having devoted several weeks in completing a work to contribute to the celebration of a great public event, feels anxious, not to solicit, but to urge his claim to that public approbation which constitutes his only reward. Let him then be permitted to suggest, that what he now offers to the world is an attempt, at least, at legitimate, original comedy; that its chief and obvious design, however imperfectly executed, may entitle it to the indulgence, if not the favor of every friend to America and to freedom; that of the principal characters, which belong rather to general than local nature, two or three are wholly or in a great measure new to the stage, though well known in the world; and that none of the mirth or praise which the piece may excite can be justly attributed to any extravagant complication of incidents, any caricatured portraiture of human nature, nor any of the tricks or contrivances by which dulness so often courts and obtains the applause of folly.

To the Managers of the Charleston Theatre[4] the author's thanks are due. for their continued attention in getting up the piece. He owes to Mr. Hodgkinson, in particular, a distinct and strong acknowledgement, for the ability and unremitted care which he employed, and the anxious zeal which he evinced for the play's success; to which his exertions as an actor as well as a manager essentially contributed......His performance was every thing that could have been desired; easy and natural, though distinguished for constant and unabated vivacity and energy....He drew the prominent figure

4. Located in Charleston, South Carolina, this venue was the nexus for dramatic production in the early Republican South.

he had to delineate with a hold but correct pencil; the colouring was throughout rich and vivid, never taudry or glaring. Mr. Sully too pourtrayed the Spanish judge in a masterly style; representing the several features by which that character is marked, with accurate and forcible discrimination, and frequently reminding those who had seen Parsons, of some of the happiest peculiarities of that celebrated comedian. Mr. Turn-bull did justice to M'Gregor. The platonic lady of Mrs. Placide was, in every respect, judicious, animated and elegant. Mrs. Brett likewise conceived the part of Theresa perfectly, and gave it with a degree of sprightliness and spirit which would have done credit to the best actress on any stage. Mrs. Villiers and Mrs. Marshall merit great commendation also for the excellence of their respective performances.

Dramatis Personæ

Don Bertoldo de la Plata, ...Mr. Sully.

Phelim O'Flinn, ...Mr. Hodgkinson.

Sawny M'Gregor, ...Mr. Turnbull.

Captain O'Brien, ...Mr. Cromwell.

Father Francisco, ...Mr. Perkins.

Don Antonio Gaspar, ...Mr. Poe.[5]

Don Rodriquez, ...Mr. Dykes.

Don Joseph, ...Mr. Charnock.

Fairtrade, ...Mr. Hughes.

American General, ...Mr. Whitlock.

French Prefect,[6] ....Mr. Placide.

Scrivana, ...Mr. West.

Soldiers, Alguazils, Servants,

Senora de la Plata, ... Mrs. Placide.

Laura, ... Mrs. Villiers.

Theresa, ... Mrs. Brett.

Lucy Margland, ... Mrs. G. Marshal.

Widow Sanchez, ... Mrs. Turnbull.

5. David Poe Jr., father of Edgar Allan Poe.
6. Governor.

LIBERTY IN LOUISIANA;

A COMEDY

ACT I.

*SCENE—A Wood near the banks of the river Mississippi;
a distant view of the city of New Orleans.*

PHELIM O'FLINN, *(without.)* HOLLOA! holloa! holloa! Sawny M'Gregor, and be damned to you, my dear! *(Enter* PHELIM, *looking around.)* Where are you, Sawny? If you have lost your-self, why don't you tell me where you are? *(pulls out a flask and drinks.)* Oh! I must take a drop of comfort, before I search any farther! *(Sings—Tune,* Oh my kitten.[7])

> And its oh, my whisky, my whisky,
>   And oh, my whisky, my honey!
> The de'il a thing makes one so frisky
>   That was ever yet bought with money.
> To the noddle it rises up up,
>   As the throat it goes down down downy;
> And when we have swigg'd a good sup,
>   We begin to reel round roundy.
> They may talk of their claret and sherry,
>   Their Burgundy, hock and Madeira;
> But to make me quite happy and merry,
>   Oh, whisky, its you are my deary.
> For it gets to my noddle up up,
>   As my throat it goes down down downy,
> And when I have swigg'd a good sup,
>   I begin to reel round round remedy.

---

7. A British nursery rhyme from the 1800s. See *Mother Goose's Melody: or, Sonnets for the Cradle. In Two Parts*. (London: John Newberry, 1765).

Holloa! Sawny, my brave lump of a fellow! Where the devil has he thrust himself? Twenty to one now he has put down his pedlar's pack, and crammed himself into the hollow of some old tree, to rest himself and count over his money. That's a very low way that Sawny has got—Forty times a day he reckons his dollars, and fingers them over and over again; and with his Scotch brogue, that no one can understand, counts yan, twa, three. Well, this money reckoning's a sort of a main dirty trick I was never much given to in my life—To be sure I never had much, by my soul, to reckon. Why, Sawny! May be the blackguard's asleep, and pritends not to hear me. Sawny M'Gregor, I say!—I suppose he has passed on forward, and will he here by and by; so I'll wait for him. (*birds heard singing.*) Hark! tweet, tweet, tweet! Devil burn me if I havn't got into the middle of a rookery of linnets and nightingales. Their singing is as delightful for myself to hear as the notes of a young pig just killing for supper. What can have become of Sawny? I must look about for him.

[*Exit, searching and singing.*

Enter SAWNY M'GREGOR, *at the other side, with a pedlar's pack on his back.*

SAWNY. The de'il tak ye, Mr. Phelim O'Flinn. Where can he hae pack'd himsel'? I hae luk'd up and down for ye; and ca'd alood till my lungs crack'd again, like a bag-pipe bursting wi' over muckle wind. What a curs'd fule this maister O'Flinn is! Ay, gude troth, and a wee bit of a knave. For a' that he has a pleas-ant guidly disposition—he'll fight brawley, but he hates the laws, and acts as if there was nae sic a thing as property. He's a devilish gude companion though. Mony a hungry weam[8] should we baith hae had, gin Phelim were as delicate about taking other people's property as Sawny M'Gregor is—I'd fast till I was famished afore I wad nock a goose or a bublie-jock[9] on the head, and put it into my poke, as Phelim does—for I'm very honest; though I dinna ken ony sin in taking share on't, when roasted, to satisfy the cravings o' nature.

8. (Scottish dialect) stomach.
9. (Scottish dialect) a turkey.

PHELIM, (*without.*) Sawny M'Gregor! Sawny M'Gregor!

SAWNY. There's the loon, bellowing like a great Irish bull, as he is. Holloa! Phelim! here I am.

Enter PHELIM.

PHELIM. Oh, the devil sweep you, Sawny; is that yourself? Why didn't you let me know where you were? Sure if you fell asleep by accident, it would be aisy for you to call out to me first, and tell me so.

SAWNY. Why, ye loon, I've been looking about for ye this half hour. I thought ye had started a lassie, or had got in pursuit of a goose or a pig for dinner.

PHELIM. No, Sawny, I intend to pay a visit to that big house yonder, near the city, and invite you and myself to dine there.

SAWNY. You hae impudence enough to do ony thing.

PHELIM. Oh! its only a little modest assurance—Would it not be a shame to go into such a fine plentiful city as New-Orleans on an empty stomach, especially on the day the Americans take possession of it?

SAWNY. You are very fond o' the American law, Phelim, ant you!

PHELIM. By my soul, honey, I ask your pardon; it never was fond of me, and I wish the devil had it and every other law in the world into the bargain.

SAWNY. Phelim we should do but badly without law.

PHELIM. A great deal better than with it Sawny. If the Congress, good luck to them, instead of turning out a few of the Judges awhile ago, had just sent all the blackguards together about their business, a man might live in peace and security, help himself to whatever he fancied, and leather any one he lik'd. (*drinks.*)

SAWNY. You'll ne'er do any guid for yersel; maister Phelim, tul ye
gie up sic notions, and tul ye drink less whisky; if it was nae for
that, ye might hae still kept your good profitable grog-shop at
the Natchez, instead o' being obliged to run awa, and leave a'
your liquors to be seiz'd by the sheriff.

PHELIM. Be aisy—Devil a thing will he find, but empty casks and
bottles. Do you think myself could have had the heart to leave
them if there was any thing good in them? Here's to you,
Sawny, (*drinks*)—I'll warrant we'll get something good in that
same fine house before we leave it.

SAWNY. Vary likely! Perhaps I may sell some o' my goods there.

PHELIM. Devil sweep you, honey! You never can get the pedlar out
of your head, no more nor myself can throw the jontleman off
my back.

SAWNY. You're a great fule, maister Phelim; but hearken to me—
When we get to this same fine house, look about vary warily,
and gin ye can see any opening for a fair stratagem to put the
siller into our pouches, dunna miss it; but it munna be dishonest, you ken.

PHELIM. A money-drawer lying open, or a silver tea-pot going
astray. (*Jeeringly.*)

SAWNY. Hoot, awa, mon! hoot, awa, mon! never steal, gin ye can get
siller honestly—above a', dunna steal ony thing that the owner
may ken again when he sees it. To be sure, a mon need na be
sae parteecular about siller in coin, for nobody can ca' it his ain,
but he that has it in his bond. But I never like to do what's not
just, for I'm very honest.

PHELIM. Leave off now, Mr. Sawny! You're always bothering about
being just, and what not. You've a great deal of honesty in your
mouth, but mighty little of it any where else. Don't pester us so
much about it.

DUET.—*Phelim.*

Arrah, Sawny, give over your blarny and brogues,
    What we can't help to do sure we must;
If the wants of the flesh didn't make us such rogues
    'Twould be aisy enough to be just.

If myself was not always so damnably poor,
    Devil burn me if ever I'd cheat;
Nor of jail would brave Phelim go inside the door,
    Could he live without clothes, drink and meat.

Sawny.

Since we canna provide for the back and the maw,
    Without cash to buy meat, drink and clothes;
Get cash by all means, but tak care o' the *law*.
    And ne'er cheat—except under the rose.[10]

PHELIM. Well said, honest Sawny; come along and let us see who
can do best in a good honest way.

            [Exeunt.

SCENE—*Theresa's Apartment, in the house of*
DON BERTOLDO DE LA PLATA.

THERESA, *(alone.)* What a plague it is to manage the family of another. All the trouble, without any of the sweets of matrimony!
If one were in that blissful state, indeed, and with a flock of
dear little babes about one, there would be some comfort for
one's toil; but to be house-keeper to anyone, and above all to a
Spanish Judge like Don Bertoldo, who is as great an epicure as
an archbishop—Why, one might as well be cook to a monas-
tery of friars. And then the old fool's love for his ward Donna

---

10. "Under the rose" is a literal English translation of the Latin phrase *sub rosa*, re-
ferring to something done in secret or undercover.

Laura, makes him so jealous of letting any agreeable young fellows into the house, that it's almost as bad as if one lived in a nunnery—not the least chance for a husband! What, though I am treated rather like a friend and companion than a house-keeper; I'd have them to know, that better blood runs in my veins than they can boast of—Marry come up, indeed! The daughter of Captain Emanuel Felix Xavier Anthonio Ferdinand Armadillo is company for the best judge in Old Spain; not to talk of a colonial alcalde,[11] the son of a Sevillian alguazil.[12] But here comes the old fool himself, and Laura, as usual, along with him.

Enter DON BERTOLDO, leading in LAURA.

DON BERTOLDO. Good morning, good Theresa; I come to tell you to give directions that we may dine early to-day. I have a particular reason for it; and let us have something nice, if you please.

THERESA Yes, Senor, I always take care of that—because I know—

DON BERTOLDO. Not, Theresa, that I care what I eat; my vigorous constitution (*coughs*) and manly habits (*coughs*) make me indifferent to such things. Besides, being in the very prime of life, it would be a shame for me to think about them.

THERESA. True, Senor.

DON BERTOLDO. But you know, worthy Theresa, it is entirely on my dear ward's account that I am anxious.

THERESA. Certainly, Senor—(*aside*) Devil's in his assurance.

DON BERTOLDO. So, Theresa, let us have something nice for her. As for me, a little turtle-soup, a stewed rock-fish, a haunch of Kentucky venison, a mince of rice-birds' breasts and a marrow pudding, and a plague of all your nice dishes, I say. Then,

11. Spanish judge.
12. Also spelled "alguacil," a Spanish law officer.

with a little old hock and seltzer water, half a dozen glasses of Champaigne, a bottle of humble *cote roti*, a few bunches of grapes and a plate of olives, I shall be able to make up my dinner. Temperance! oh, temperance! it is the richest jewel of life! the handmaid of health; the preserver of manhood; the parent and the nurse of love! (*pressing Laura's hand, and looking ridiculously on her.*)

Enter Senora de la Plata, *unobserved by* Don Bertoldo.

Senora de la Plata. Indeed, Senor Glutton! (*Bertoldo starts.*) Bless me, Senor, you have become exceedingly fond of your ward of late!

Don Bertoldo. Every one must be fond of her, madam.

Senora de la Plata. Always with her—always praising her beauties; and, like a tender physician, always feeling her pulse.

Don Bertoldo. Well, madam! and why not?

Senora de la Plata. When she is present, lost in contemplation of her, you forget yourself. Yes, strange to tell, you forget your great age and your numerous infirmities.

Don Bertoldo. Zounds! Senora!

Senora de la Plata. Gout, rheumatism, catarrh!

Don Bertoldo. Senora! silence, I charge you. Remember the respect due to Don Bertoldo de la Plata.

Laura. I entreat, Senor.

Don Bertoldo. I say, madam, I have not yet pass'd the middle age of life.

Senora de la Plata. Certainly, Senor, if you have been ordained to live to the age of one hundred and thirty. (*laughing.*)

Don Bertoldo. It is true that the climate of this country has occasioned me some slight indispositions—but these always attack young persons like me, who reside here.

Senora de la Plata. Climate, indeed! Twenty-two years ago, when you paid your addresses to me, you told me just the same thing to account for your strange appearance, even at that time. You said you had been a soldier at Manilla; that your legs had been spindled by a plague; that your face had been wrinkled up by your accidentally falling asleep under a poison tree. You were then upwards of forty years of age, and owned to thirty-two.

Don Bertoldo. By the integrity of a Spanish Judge, I swear it is false, (*appears uneasy.*) Laura, my dear, retire; it will be painful to you to listen to this woman's impertinence. (*leads her to the door.*) Theresa, you may accompany Donna Laura. (*Exeunt Laura and Theresa.*)—I am old, eh! Well, then, let me put on my spectacles to view this nonpareil of youth, grace and beauty, who was married twenty-two years ago. (*puts on spectacles.*)

Senora de la Plata. I was then but fourteen years of age, when my father compelled me—

Don Bertoldo. Indeed! Why your lover, Don Felix Furioso, had been two years before banished to South-America for killing the Corregidor's son, as he leaped out of your chamber window.

Senora de la Plata Ah, Senor, (*weeps*) why do you bring to my soul such cruel recollections? Why remind me of what I suffered from the pure and platonic affection I entertained for that amiable, that noble youth?

Don Bertoldo. Affections of the same celestial kind, I presume, as you have conceived for that American-Irishman, Captain O'Brien, whom you met with at Mons. Bordell's, when you and Laura were up the river on a visit.

Senora de la Plata. Ah, Senor—no one could contemplate such an object—a brilliant gem of human nature, polished as the oriental topaz—a soul sublimated to the highest heaven of enthusiasm, and the exquisite pleasures of platonic love—No one, my dear Senor, could see such an object as O'Brien without feeling friendship for him.

Don Bertoldo. Friendship—platonic friendship. (*ironically.*)

Senora de la Plata. Yes, Senor—immaculate and intellectual as the loves of angels; or, as I have beautifully expressed it in a delicious sonnet—

"My soul luxuriates in seraphic love,
"Spotless and pure—as a platonic dove."

Don Bertoldo. Ti-*ti*-tum, *ti*-tum, *ti*-tum, *ti*! And this empyrean affection met, I trust, a suitable return?

Senora de la Plata. Why, yes, Senor; but it was the beauty of my mind alone which that tasteful and intelligent youth admired—for you know, my dear Don Bertoldo, I have an exquisite taste in the elegant arts; wonderful felicities in the composition of amatory poems; the most engaging and fascinating manners; in a word, all the taste, the grace and elegance of the old court—

Don Bertoldo. Together with all that is excellent and lovely in the morals of the new. (*ironically.*)

Senora de la Plata. Yes, Senor, such morals as do no discredit to Don Bertoldo de la Plata.

Don Bertoldo. To me, madam! What do you mean? I am integrity itself.

Senora de la Plata. Ha, ha, ha! Be not offended, I entreat you. Indeed, my love, I do not wish to wound your delicate and sensitive moral nerves, but merely to suggest to your worship's wisdom, that nothing can be more ridiculous than insinuations against any one's moral character, coming from you. But you must know, my dear, that I have something to say to you of importance.

Don Bertoldo. What is it, madam?

Senora de la Plata. *(after a short pause.)* You know, my love, it need not be concealed—we hate each other cordially.

Don Bertoldo. Most cordially, indeed, my love!

Senora de la Plata. And each of us, my dear, prefers any one's society to that of the other.

Don Bertoldo. Very true, indeed, my dear—To speak for myself, I consider my *better* half the *worst* company in the world.

Senora de la Plata. Very candid, my dear. There is nothing so amiable as perfect candor.

Don Bertoldo. Nothing, my love.

Senora de la Plata. Jealousy, my dear, as you have long been convinced, is a foolish and wicked passion.

Don Bertoldo. Indeed I have, my dear; and though a Spaniard, I am perfectly innocent of it. If any thing like it ever appeared in my conduct, it was merely feigned, for the purpose of giving to my lovely consort the delightful feeling produced by a little occasional vexation, thrown in to vary the otherwise insipid monotony of her happy life.

Senora de la Plata. *(aside.)* Hideous creature!

Don Bertoldo. To operate like those discords in fine music, which heighten the charm of the harmonious passages that follow them.

Senora de la Plata. Kind Sir!

Don Bertoldo. And also, my love, to improve your beauty; for nothing gives such a fine crimson to the dimpled cheek, or such a vivid lustre to the rolling eye, as a fit of rage. So that the more angry I could make you, my love, the more beautiful you would appear.

SENORA DE LA PLATA. Excellent—Your good understanding, as well as your candor, at once instructs and charms me.

DON BERTOLDO. Well, then, that I may render myself more deserving of your compliments, I must acknowledge, that I feel as great a friendship for Laura, as you can do for O'Brien—full as pure—full as platonic.

SENORA DE LA PLATA. *(aside.)* Cupid on crutches!—*(aloud)*—Admirable—I declare I'll celebrate you both in my immortal poetry, under the name of 'The Petrarch and Laura of Louisiana!'[13] And when your worship dies, (Heaven avert the fatal day!) I'll compose a most pathetic epitaph on the mournful occasion. Nay, I'll have a fountain, as renowned as the Vaucluse[14] itself, erected, to perpetuate the remembrance of your loves, in the middle of your own rice swamp. Ha, ha, ha!

DON BERTOLDO. Thank you, my dear; thank you for your kind intentions.

SENORA How lovely, my dear, is the divinity of truth! How amply it furnishes its votaries with the means of obtaining a virtuous felicity! I think, my love, we now understand each other well.

DON BERTOLDO. Yes, my dear lady, without the least reserve—alike we know each other, and alike we love.

SENORA DE LA PLATA. Then attend. The last time I was in company with Captain O'Brien, Laura was of the party—

DON BERTOLDO. Eh! what?

SENORA DE LA PLATA. And before she left it became, if I am not much mistaken, deeply enamoured of him.

---

13. Francesco Petrarca (1307–1374), commonly known as Petrarch, was an Italian poet who created the sonnet and wrote a sonnet sequence to a woman he called "Laura."

14. The Fontaine de Vaucluse is a natural karst spring in southern France and one of the largest in the world.

DON BERTOLDO. Hell and the devil!

SENORA DE LA PLATA. He seemed not altogether insensible. The nobler and mental charms of another person *(with affected vanity)* had indeed done full justice to your taste, my dear; but my quick and acute discernment soon discovered that his passions were contending against his judgment and his taste; that his soul, in short, was not wholly purified from all anti-platonic emotions.

DON BERTOLDO. No wonder, my love, when Laura was before him.

SENORA DE LA PLATA. Detested creature! *(aside)*—In a word, my life, Laura is young and beautiful, and for a child, has a tolerable engaging manner. It is known too that she is entitled to a large fortune. To-morrow, it is said, the Americans, and with them Captain O'Brien, will come to take possession of New-Orleans. Now, if my conjectures; are right, and I am very confident they are, the young man may think that Laura's fortune would compensate for her intellectual inferiority. To be plain, my dearest, her platonic friendship would be lost to you for ever.

DON BERTOLDO. And you, my love, would be for ever deprived of the virtuous conversation of Captain O'Brien!

SENORA DE LA PLATA. Suppose, then, my soul's idol, you set off immediately to the Havanna,[15] and take Laura along with you.

DON BERTOLDO. An excellent thought. *(calmly.)*

SENORA DE LA PLATA. Or to Spain, if you choose—Its delightful climate may perhaps remove some of your infirmities. And I might remain here, my love, to take care of our property.

DON BERTOLDO. And the modest young Irishman would assist my beloved in the management of it.

---

15. Havana, Cuba.

SENORA DE LA PLATA. And then, darling of my heart, we should effectually separate these lovers for ever, *(aside)* and I should soon be able to obtain a divorce and marry O'Brien.

DON BERTOLDO. So we should, my love!—*(aside)* for which reason I have already determined to do what you propose—and then I dare swear you will soon enable me to obtain a divorce and marry Laura.

SENORA DE LA PLATA. Oh, you dear, charming—*(aside)* hideous old dotard—But I see Laura returning—Direct her to be ready to go by the frigate that sails this evening.

DON BERTOLDO. Yes, my dear, yes.

SENORA DE LA PLATA. I don't wish that O'Brien should see her again. Meet me presently in the boudoir, to arrange matters further. Adieu! charmer of my existence! How shall I collect fortitude to part with you so soon, perhaps for ever! *(pretends to weep, and then bursts out into a laugh.)*

[*Exit.*

DON BERTOLDO. *(solus)* Ha, ha, ha! Your plan, my good platonist, has been already arranged by me. I did not wait for your advice before I determined on taking Laura to Europe, and leaving your ladyship behind. You shall have full powers to manage my property here, if you can find any—All that I possessed in this province is already sold, and the proceeds safely lodged in the Havanna. In love with O'Brien! Ha, ha, ha!—The flash that has touched her dry withered heart may, like a spark of fire from a flint into a tinder-box, burn a little, and smoke without doing much mischief. It shall serve, however, to light the torch that Cupid and Hymen[16] are preparing for me and my dear little Laura! Delightful, transporting, ravishing thought.

16. Cupid was the Roman god of love, and Hymen, the Roman god of marriage.

Song, **Don Bertoldo**—*Air,* Black Joke.[17]

If I can my platonic consort deceive,
Or plump her at once down six feet in the grave,
    Oh, what a joke and prospect so bright!
As Europa, by Jove, I'll lead Laura away
Over seas;[18] where I'll kiss and make love night and day,
Spend the whole of our time in soft dalliance and play,
Till subdu'd by my fondness, she'll tenderly say,
    Oh, what a joke and prospect so bright!

Should madam take up with her Captain O'Brien,
While at him people laugh, and herself they cry fie on,
    Oh, what a joke and prospect so bright!
I'll get a divorce, and my sweet Laura tether,
In wedlock's soft hands—then, like birds of a feather,
As two turtles we'll bill, coo and cling close together,
To drive off cold winter, and keep out the weather,
    Oh, the dear joke and prospect so bright!

Then fly swift, ye moments, and to my fond arms
Bring Laura, with her irresistible charms;
    Oh, what a prospect pleasing and bright!
While my lady so prim, like a piece of crack'd delf,
Shall lie unregarded by me on the shelf,
My Laura's rich treasures I'll take to myself,
Her sweet person pillage and pocket her pelf,
    Oh, Lord, what a joke and prospect so bright!

Enter **Laura** *and* **Theresa.**

Don Bertoldo. (*taking Laura the hand.*) Laura, my love, you must prepare immediately for our voyage to the Havanna.

---

17. A lewd song common in England and Ireland in the 1700s.

18. In Greek mythology, Europa was a princess of Tyre, whom the chief god Zeus, as a bull, courted. Eventually he kidnapped her, bringing the woman to the island of Crete, where she delivered three sons: Sarpedon, Rhadamanthus, and Minos. According to the myth, Europe is named for her.

LAURA. For the Havanna?

DON BERTOLDO. Yes; why should it surprise you? Have you not heard that the Americans are expected to take possession of this place to-morrow.

LAURA. I have, Senor—But surely that circumstance need not hasten our departure.

DON BERTOLDO. A frigate waits, my child, only for us.

LAURA. Will there not be several other opportunities of going to Cuba in a little time hence?

DON BERTOLDO. None so safe and agreeable as that which now offers. But why, my Laura, are you unwilling to go there now?

LAURA. (*hesitating*) Why, Senor, I shall not have time to take leave of my friends. I have many beloved companions of my childhood in this country.

DON BERTOLDO. (*aside*) My lynx-ey'd platonist is right. Laura must be got off before O'Brien appears—(*aloud*) Aye, aye—but you'll soon see all your friends in the Havanna. They won't remain here long, under the odious American government.

LAURA. I thought, sir, it had been generally approved of, as being well suited to the habits, opinions and circumstances of the people who live under it.

DON BERTOLDO. Nonsense, my dear, nonsense. Whenever men are free, they get so fat and saucy, there's no bearing them. Did you not hear, Theresa, how that Kentucky rascal abused me the other day, for only insisting on having a few barrels of his provisions at my own price? And when I threatened to chastise him with my cane for his impertinence, the impudent villain immediately presented his rifle, and laughed and mocked at me.

THERESA. So he did, your worship—And he said with a terrible oath—"Take care, (*mimicking the back-country pronunciation*) you mister; for if you put your gouty foot into my boat, nation to me if I don't shoot out your two remaining rotten old grinders—and save you the expence of tooth-drawing."

DON BERTOLDO. Damn him, woman; don't repeat his impertinent lies. I hope you have made up your mind to depart with us; you won't think of remaining among such savages, surely?

THERESA. I ask your worship's pardon. I have no great objection to see the young fellows free, fat and hearty; aye, by my conscience and pretty forward too.

DON BERTOLDO. Experience will make you wiser, child.

THERESA. Does Senora la Plata accompany us?

DON BERTOLDO. No, my dear. She remains here for a short time to settle my affairs; but she will follow us speedily. We have no time to lose. Theresa, let every thing he prepared for my departure.

[*Exit.*

LAURA *and* THERESA—*Laura seems thoughtful and melancholy.*

THERESA. Why, lady, what is the matter with you?

LAURA. Ah, my dear Theresa, this order for my immediate departure, and it seems without the Senora, too much confirms me in the suspicions I have just hinted to you.

THERESA. So it does me, my dear young lady. I see clearly what these wretches are about. Captain O'Brien and you are to be separated for their wicked purposes.

LAURA. I fear that is their intention.

THERESA. But do you really believe he loves you?

LAURA. He told me so, with every appearance of sincerity.

THERESA. Oh, deuce take the sincerity of the best of them. I have been so often left in the lurch myself, that—

LAURA. Yes, but Theresa, he has since declared it in a letter, professing in the most earnest, yet delicate language, the ardor and fidelity of his affection for me.

THERESA. It may be so—But you should be sure of it, before you let your mind be too far engaged—If I had been mere cautious myself, my tender heart would have been spared many a twinge—worse a hundred times than the rheumatism.

LAURA. (*pausing*) Why, I do recollect—I do recollect that almost the whole of his respect and attentions were directed, during our interview, to Senora la Plata.

THERESA. That, however, makes the business look better—It is clear he could not love one so much older than himself (*affectedly*) as my lady. His attentions to her must then have been intended as a cover to hide his addresses to you, and to secure a future intercourse with you. I dare say he soon discovered her fondness for what she calls fashionable platonic love-making. Now, for my part, I don't like your new-fangled ways—old-fashioned love is quite good enough for Theresa.

LAURA. His eyes, indeed, seemed paying addresses to me, while his tongue flattered her.

THERESA. I'll warrant me. You may always trust Theresa in things of this sort—I have had some experience in them, lady.

LAURA. But what I most apprehend is, that an attachment arising from a single interview may not be sincere or lasting.

THERESA. Tell me, truly, do you love this young gentleman yourself?

LAURA. Why, Theresa, I really believe I should, if I were only certain that he loved me.

THERESA. And why will you not give him credit for being as sincere as yourself?

LAURA. To be sure, if ever character was faithfully displayed by the human countenance, the heart of O'Brien is kind, generous and true.

THERESA. And I dare say he can draw from your countenance, young lady, just as fond and as faithful a picture of your disposition.

LAURA. If I am mistaken, Theresa, I'll go into the first convent I meet with.

THERESA. Ah! a convent—fie, fie!—out upon the hideous notion. A convent indeed!—A jail, a purgatory sooner. No, no, my dear, neither of us was ever intended for such a place. Out upon it! Give me for my money a kind, hearty, good-humoured husband.

LAURA. Indeed!

THERESA. Yes, indeed—active, generous, and faithful as a spaniel dog; and, by my faith, as submissive too. Such a man, with a parcel of prattling children and jovial neighbors, are much pleasanter company than old maiden nuns.

LAURA. Children, Theresa!

THERESA. Aye, lady, the more the merrier; for then one never wants society. And now, my dear child, let me ask if the captain knows that you have a large fortune?

LAURA. He thinks I have none. I told him so myself, in the course of conversation, and the Senora instantly corroborated it with great earnestness.

THERESA. Was it afterwards that he wrote you that handsome love-letter?

LAURA. It was.

THERESA. Then, my blessings on him. A very good sign, upon my word; and, give me leave to tell you, a very extraordinary one. Money is now-a-days as requisite for marriage as for market— one can get nothing that's toothsome in either with an empty purse. I'm sure if merit without fortune would have satisfied the men, and be-whipp'd to them, I should have been a wife and a mother long ago. I would give a little bag of doubloons myself to have a young lover I could depend upon, so well as you may on Capt. O'Brien.

LAURA. But what signifies his sincerity, if Don Bertoldo obliges me to leave the province?

THERESA. Don't be afraid of that old baboon. This day, perhaps, your dear captain will be here to protect you.

LAURA. In his letter he mentions that he does not expect he shall be able to be here till to-morrow.

THERESA. That will do. Indeed, I require protection myself as much as any one. I am so afraid that some of those tall, strong Kentucky *crackers*, (as they call them) who frequently pay us a visit as they are passing down the river, should take it into their heads to run away with me.

LAURA. I hope, my good old and faithful friend, there's no danger.

THERESA. But I tell you there is great danger—I wonder I have escaped so long. Old, quoth'a!—Let me tell you, miss, that Theresa Armadillo can not be called an old woman till five and twenty years more shall pass away—and, please the Virgin, she shan't be called an old maid then. No danger, indeed! No one is in greater. My very heart goes pit-a-pat, and my whole person becomes agitated, whenever one of those strapping back-woods fellows comes in my sight.

LAURA. Well, good Theresa, I hope none of them will injure you.

THERESA. By my troth, lady. I am no more safe than my neighbors. Old as you think me, however, I expect to dance very merrily at your wedding, and that too in a short time, please the Virgin.

LAURA. And I hope, kind Theresa, I shall soon rejoice at your's.

[Exit.

THERESA. Heaven grant it, my dear child.——And now to see that every thing is prepared for dinner.

[Exit into an inner apartment.

ACT II.

The same scene.

Enter **PHELIM** *and* **SAWNY**—*Sawny looking round very cautiously.*

SAWNY. In troth, Phelim, here is a gudlely hoose. I dare say the maister of it is rich. Wha knows but they'll buy up a' my goods. This, I tak it, is the great mon's hoosekeeper's room.

PHELIM, (*going towards a closet*) By my soul, Sawny, if my noes isn't a great liar, we'll soon see something very savoury in the ateing way. (*finds a tureen of turtle-soup.*)

SAWNY. Tak heed, mon! ma' be you think so only because your weam is empty, and your heed fu'.

PHELIM. Holy St. Patrick! What a flagrant smell.

SAWNY. (*examining cautiously*) Gude troth, it has a deleecious flavour!

PHELIM. Phelim is seldom mistaken when he makes a good guess.

SAWNY. What is it, laddie?

PHELIM. I believe its a sort of a savoury stirabout,[19] made of meat.

SAWNY. Why, ye loon, its turtle-soup.

PHELIM. Whatever it is, I'll taste a little of it. (*helps himself.*)

SAWNY. (*aside*) I'd like to ha' a taste too. (*To Phelim*) You're always too free, mon, in helping yoursel'. Dunna you ken hoo many

---

19. Stirabout is an oat- or corn-based porridge mixed with milk or water, then boiled and stirred. This reference is a jab at Phelim's poor, Irish background.

scrapes you got us baith into by taking sic leeberties, on oor journey frae New-York to the Natchez?

PHELIM. Oh, my dear, wern't we then in a land of liberty, and where else ought a man to make free? Did I ever take any thing but in a fair, open, jontlemanlike way? And if I brought you now and then into a scrape, didn't I always get you handsomely out of it?

SAWNY. And ha' na I got you, maister Phelim, out of mony a scrape? Dunna you remember when you were put in jail in New-York for debt, where you might ha' lain till now, gin I had na put it into your heed to tak the yellow fever and die? Did na I, when every one besides was afraid to gang near you, go with an undertaker, and carry you oot safe and sound?

PHELIM. Aye, by my soul, and almost smothered me in the coffin, for want of making the air-holes large enough. Devil burn me if ever I'll die again of the yellow fever as long as 1 live, unless I can't help it. But have not I risked, aye, by my soul, and got too, many a leathering on your account, Sawny?

SAWNY. Why, you dunna want for spunk, Phelim, to be sure; but you'd be a better mon and a safer companion, gin you did na tak what you wanted till you had the owner's permeesion.

PHELIM. By my soul, honest Phelim would rather any day take a thing like a jontleman, nor beg for it like a spalpeen; and he's always as ready to give to a poor body, as to borrow from a churl that's rich.

SAWNY. It costs leetle to say so, maister Phelim, when a mon has nathing to give; but gin you were as generous as you say you are, it is na right to be so at other folks' expence.

PHELIM. I tell you, Sawny, it is—and for why? Sure if any one finds fault with me, am not I always ready to give him *satisfaction*; and what can any raisonable person desire more? Don't you know the rich blackguard we had the scuffle with on the borders of the Tennessee wilderness?

SAWNY. He that ca'd us a pair of impudent rascals, for roasting one of his turkies and drinking half a gallon of his whusky, when he was absent, and without asking ony one's leave?

PHELIM. The same. Tho' I tould him I thought it would be affronting American hospitality for a jontleman not to make as free in any American's house as in his own, he grumbled and abused me; and then because I only laughed at him, he insisted on satisfaction; which, to be sure, he got, in as neat a leathering as ever I gave in my born days. What could I do more, Sawny?

SAWNY. Troth, I think you did too much.

PHELIM. Sawny, you don't know the ways of jontlemen yet, though you've kept company so long with me. I tell you, that whenever a jontleman does wrong, its a complete satisfaction and reparation if he afterwards shoots or leathers the man that he has injured.

SAWNY. Oh, you wicked sinner!

PHELIM. Oh! now, Sawny, with all your fine preaching, you're not ashamed, by my soul, to benefit by what you censure so much. The best part of the ateing of that very turkey came to your share, while the whole of the bateing afterwards fell to mine— There's not much conscience in your stomach, my dear.

SAWNY. The whole of the beating, and confound ye!—I tell ye what, maister Phelim, gin ye think I'm at a' afraid of a beating, come oot wi me into the wood, and I'll try if I canna rattle the shillelah, as ye ca' it, aboot your ears tul ye change your opeenion.

PHELIM. Now, do you think, my brave laddie, I can doubt your spunk, when we have so often fought for one another? No, by my soul; you're always as ready to fight as myself, right or wrong, and that's saying no little in your praise.

SAWNY. Especially, Phelim, when there's ony thing to be gained by it—I dunna care much to ha' what ye ca' (*imitating*) a leathering, just for divarsion. He's a silly cheel that gets broken bones for nathing; but he's a sorry dog that wul na fight for a bone.

PHELIM. I like you very well, lad, if you didn't talk so much about your honesty and your conscience; when, by my soul, you can chate as roundly as the best of us. To be sure, you have always the law of your side, devil burn you.

SAWNY. Aye, Phelim, what I do is always in the way o' fair trade, as an honest, conscientious pedlar. I never sell ony thing for gold that is not trebble gilt, and seldom ask a greater profit than a thoosand per cent.

PHELIM. Let me tell you, Sawny, the devil an honester fellow in America than Phelim O'Flinn.

SAWNY. Except in leetle money matters, debts and the like.

PHELIM. Don't be after giving us so much of your blarney. As to money matters, I tell you no one loves generosity more nor myself.

SAWNY. Vary good poleecy, Phelim; ye may gain but canna lose by it.

PHELIM. Be aisy now—and as to debts, I'm always willing to do as I'd be done by, and what can be fairer. I'd frealy give to every one that owes me any money a resalt in full, and all I ask of my creditors is to do the same by honest Phelim O'Flinn; but they won't, the curs'd knaves—they are always sending their sheriffs and constables after me, and putting me to the trouble and expence of swearing out and white-washing two or three times every year.

SAWNY. Sure enough, they're vary troublesome; and I fear it will never be better while ye stick to the dram-selling business. Gin ye'd tak a fule's advice, ye'd hae na mare to do wi' it.

PHELIM. By my soul, Sawny, that's the business that will suit me best; for while I'm in it, I'll always be sure of *one* good customer at least—myself.—But come now, let us attack the savoury stew again, (*sits down and eats.*)

SAWNY. Hark! Some one comes this way. Tak heed, mon!

Enter THERESA *from the inner apartment.*

THERESA, (*aside*) Ha! who have we got here?

(*Sawny bows very low, and retires into a corner.*)

PHELIM. (*rising from his seat and lifting up his hands in admiration*)
Oh! Sawny, my dream is out!—Didn't I tell you that I'd see
this very morning a beautiful sweet cratur of a dear young
jontlewoman, in just such a room as this; and that she'd bid me
welcome with a *kaith miel a faltough*, and force me, whether
I would or not, to wash down a bowl of savoury soup with a
bottle of whisky—and there now she stands before me!

(*Theresa appears astonished, but not displeased at the flattery of Phelim.*)

SONG—PHELIM.

Ogh! my lovely sweet cratur, pray how do you do?
I've been dreaming this week past of no one but you.
Give me lave to prisint to you Phelim O'Flinn,
A lad ever prepar'd to go through thick and thin.
The likes of yourself is his greatest delight,
To talk with all day, and to toy with all night.
From yourself, my dear jewel, I ne'er wish to part;
Blood-and-ouns! how your bright eyes have bother'd my heart!

THERESA. Your humble servant, gentlemen.

(*Sawny bows respectfully.*)

PHELIM. (*sits down again and eats*) You see, my dear, I'm no ways
bashful. I always like to behave myself in a genteel, hospitable
manner wherever I go.

THERESA. You are from the United States, gentlemen, I presume.

PHELIM. Yes, my dear. We are come along with the troops that we
left a few hours march behind us, just to take possession of
your country.

THERESA. I am glad they will be with us so soon. You are officers of the American government, perhaps?

PHELIM. No, my dear, not at present—we are in the mercantile line. My friend here—Give me lave to introduce him to you, Mr. Sawny M'Gregor—My friend, Sawny, is a great merchant, that has an imminse store of dry goods at the Natchez. He has brought with him a few little samples (*pointing to Sawny's pack*) to shew to his customers, the planters and small store-keepers along the river. And your humble servant, my dear, is a very rich wine and liquor merchant, from the same flourishing city; and a hearty Irishman besides; though you need not be surprised at that, for go into what country you will, you'll be sure to find Irishmen enough bred and born in it.

SAWNY. (*aside*) Weel ye ha' the deil's own impudence.

THERESA. Very reputable occupations, indeed!—Pray, gentlemen, be seated, and take some refreshment. This turtle-soup, I believe, you will find very good.

PHELIM. Come over to the table, Sawny—don't be so shame-fac'd. Let me help you. By my soul, madam, its no lie to call this soup good. The very smell of it made my own mouth water— and no wonder; for I'll warrant it was made by your own sweet self—that would make any one's mouth water.

THERESA. (*smiling*) Oh, dear, sir!—I am told, sir, the Natchez is a very delightful country.

PHELIM. Yes, my dear, very pleasant, but rather too hot for myself,

SAWNY. (*aside*) The Highlands of Scotland would be the same, gin ye liv'd there three months.

PHELIM. It's for that raison I am going to settle in New-Orleans, just for the benefit of my health.

SAWNY. (*aside*) Aye, to avoid the jail-consumption.

THERESA. Come, gentlemen, what will you drink? This is the dwelling-house of the Spanish judge, Don Bertoldo de la Plata. We have very good cheer I promise you.

PHELIM. (*aside*) A judge, eh!—That's so near a-kin to a sheriff that I like neither of them—No, by my soul, nor any thing at all belonging to the law. I suppose, my dear, you have the honor of being the judge's lady.

(Sawny rises and bows very low.)

THERESA. No, sir, I am only his worship's house-keeper; but I am treated rather as an humble friend and companion of the family than as a servant; and a good reason for it, by my conscience—I come of as good a family as the best of them.

PHELIM. I like you the better for that. I am a person of great family myself.

SAWNY. (*aside*) Vary large, in troth—You've children, I believe, in every parish in Ireland and America.

THERESA. I dare say you have both families of your own.

SAWNY. No, my lady hoose-keeper, neither of us.

THERESA. You're much in the right on't. I have no notion of people marrying too young; and for that reason I have kept myself single as yet; tho', to be sure, I might have been married, many is the hundred time. I have gained a very pretty little independency of my own in this province—a few handsome bags of doubloons in my chest, and a large fine house in New-Orleans, mighty prettily furnished; but for all that, I don't choose to marry—No, I don't choose to marry.

SAWNY. Troth, bonnie lassie, I'm vary glad to hear ye are na married yet. I ne'er met with ony one I like so muckle as yoursel. (*she curtsies.*)

PHELIM. (*aside*) Fair play, Sawny.

SAWNY. (*aside to Phelim*) Let me tak her, Phelim. Dunna thrust me awa this time, and you shall ha the doubloons—the hoose will do for me. (*to her*) Gin we were better acquainted together, lassie, I'm sure it would be a match.

THERESA. Oh, we're both young enough, sir, to think of marrying for these—three weeks to come. But, gentlemen, you have not told me what you will drink.

PHELIM. For my share, my dear, I generally drink Madeira.

SAWNY. (*aside*) Made from barley.

PHELIM. But now that I'm fatagu'd after my journey, I'd as lief have a little whiskey, if you have any in the house.

THERESA. We have some, sir, of an excellent quality, that one of my Kentucky sweethearts made me a present of.

PHELIM. By my soul, my dear cratur, if he has as good a taste for the *spirit* as for the *flesh*, his whiskey must be the best in America.

SAWNY. (*aside*) Curse the fellow. He'll tak this rich old lassie from me.

PHELIM. Nothing delights my own heart more nor to drink share of a good jug of whiskey-punch with a pretty girl.

THERESA. Sir, I love good cheer myself, especially when along with such a jovial and agreeable companion as you are.

PHELIM. Devil a handsome young jontlewoman like yourself could ever help liking an Irish boy.

SAWNY. (*aside to Phelim*) Deil tak your tongue—Leave the lassie to me, and you shall ha the doubloons and half the hoose to boot.

THERESA. Excuse me, sir, for a few minutes, while I go to the cellar and fetch a bottle of the liquor you like so much.

PHELIM. You may bring a couple of bottles, my dear, while your hand is in. [*Exit Theresa.*] (*Jeeringly*) Weel, Sawny, which of us mun tak the lassie?

SAWNY. Burn ye, canna ye let me get her—Is na the offer I made ye vary fair?

PHELIM. Ah, Sawny, honey, I only wanted to shew you that I *might* take her if I plaised—and now, to let you see how generous I am, I make her a present to you for nothing at all. No one but a young jontlewoman, by my soul, shall ever be called Mrs. Phelim O'Flinn.

SAWNY. You're a gude sort of a loon, tho' you're so conceited. The lassie has a gude riddance of ye. If she was to listen to ye, and trust ye, vary likely you'd serve her as you did Lucy Margland of Tennessee—Wasn't it a shame for ye to seduce that poor girl?

PHELIM. I vow to Jasus, I couldn't help it. The girls can never let me alone—They kidnap me whenever they can catch me, and make me list as a volunteer sweetheart whether I will or no.

SAWNY. I believe ye ha na conscience, Phelim.

PHELIM. By my troth, Sawny, you can't brag of much yourself; but you're mighty ginerous of what little you have, for, by my soul, you keep it all for other people's use. Your conscience is very quiet and aisy about your *own* roguery, tho' very squameish and particular as to your friends.

SAWNY. No, Phelim; gin I had used that innocent young lassie as ye did, I cou'd na rest tul I had married her.

PHELIM. Especially if she had ony siller—I tell you it was nothing but tinderness that prevented me from marrying her. Poor girl, she could never bear the smell of whiskey—and wouldn't it kill the dear cratur to have such a bedfellow as myself all the days of her life?

Re-enter THERESA.

THERESA. Here, gentlemen, is something to enliven us. Come, Mr. M'Gregor, make free. May I ask, sir, if you too are a native of Europe?

SAWNY. I am, gude lassie, a true-born Scot; I hope ye winna like me the less for it.

THERESA. By no means. I am very fond of the gentlemen of your country; for, by my conscience, when they get good things, they know how to take good care of them.

PHELIM. In troth, my dear, neither Mr. M'Gregor nor myself has any raison to be ashamed of our country; but sure isn't it all one, Irishman, Englishman, American or Scot—all of the same family. Now will I give you a little bit of a toast?

THERESA. With pleasure, sir—and a bumper it must be.

PHELIM. Then here's the sister nations of Ireland, England, Scotland and America—may they always live together in a brotherhood of filial affection—may they bury the enemies of their freedom in the sea, and with them the remembrance of all their own family dissentions, past, present and to come.

SAWNY. Here's the sister nations of Scotland, England, Ireland and America—freedom, prosperity and riches to them all—bankruptcy and perpetual poverty to their enemies.

THERESA. Here's the sister nations of America, England, Ireland and Scotland—freedom, prosperity and the sweet comforts of domestic happiness to them all—and conversion to their enemies.

PHELIM. But, my dear soul, its of no consequence what countryman you are, if you choose to settle in the United States; for, let you be born where you will, (do you mind) as soon as you're after being in America five years, you may become a native of it whenever you please—and good luck to the brave boys that so ginirously share their noble privileges with strangers!

THERESA. Well, gentlemen, whatever country owns you, upon my word you please me very much.

SAWNY. Vary glad, you think so, lassie; gin ye like ain of us, as weel as ain of us likes ye, troth ye winna long be a maiden.

THERESA. (*smiling affectedly*) I like you so well, gentlemen, that I'll give you a song.

SONG—THERESA.

Now Phœbus runs his glorious race,[20]
Diffusing around th' ail-cheering ray,
    And not a cloud obscures his face—
So may he shine on my bridal day.

The bridal day's the best day of our life,
    Nought then should prevail but mirth and play.
The maid should ne'er become a wife,
    Who will not rejoice on her bridal day.

SAWNY. Vary good, lassie; I like your notions mightily.

THERESA. But I had almost forgot to enquire if either of you is acquainted with Captain O'Brien, an Irish gentleman in the American service, who is expected to come here along with the troops that are to take possession of the province.

SAWNY. Mr. O'Flinn has seen him, I believe, at the Natchez.

PHELIM. Seen him, indeed! My dear, we are very intimate together. He is one of my most particular friends.
SAWNY. (*aside*) Oh, impudence!

THERESA. I wish he was come.; for you must know, as you're his friend, (but that's a secret I wouldn't tell every body) that he's

---

20. Phœbus Apollo is a Greek and Roman god who pulls the sun across the sky with his chariot every day.

over head and ears in love with Don Bertoldo's ward, Laura
de Villaverde—a charming, sweet young lady, who will have,
when she marries, a fortune of upwards of a hundred thousand dollars.

PELIM. Thunder-and-ouns!—A hundred thousand dollars!—No
wonder by my soul, he's so much in love with her!

THERESA. Aye, and the best of it is, that she's just as much in love
with him, though they have never been more than once in each
other's company.

PHELIM. (*aside*) What luck some people have in this wicked world!
No fear of the like happening to honest Phelim O'Flinn.

THERESA. I am anxious to see him. He is, as I've told you, a
countryman of your own; and indeed from the description
my young lady has given me of him, he must be very like
you in every respect—so like, that if you had not told me
who you were, I should have supposed you were Captain
O'Brien in disguise!

PHELIM. Eh?

THERESA. He is exactly of your height.

PHELIM. (*aside*) Aye! aye!

THERESA. About six or seven and twenty years old.

PHELIM. (*aside*) My own age to a single day!

THERESA. Well built and of an excellent shape.

PHELIM. (*aside*) If any one would but make me a captain now, how
aisy I might christen myself O'Brien!

THERESA. Said to be very pleasing in his manners.

PHELIM. Devil a one more so nor myself.

THERESA. Fluent and eloquent in discourse.

PHELIM. (*aside*) To be sure myself hasn't as glib a tongue as the best of them!—Phelim, take heart!—If I could pass myself for this captain, you fortune would he made forever.

THERESA. And I'm told he sings a very pleasant, lively song.

PHELIM. (*aside*) There I am again!—(*aloud*) where was it Miss Laura and he met together my dear?

THERESA. At Monsieur Bordell's plantation, up the river.

PHELIM. She saw him only once, you say?

THERESA. Once only.

PHELIM. How long is it ago?

THERESA. About a month.

PHELIM. Are you sure she'd know him again?

THERESA. I should suppose so—unless he was greatly altered.

PHELIM. (*aside*) Mayn't a man have had a smart fever and ague for the binifit of his complexion? (*aloud*) Did any one else in the house ever see my frind the Captain?

THERESA. No one but the Judge's lady, Senora de la Plata.

PHELIM. Was it often?

THERESA. Three or four times, I believe.

PHELIM. Is she ould?

THERESA. Not very old; but advancing into the vale of life.

PHELIM. And I dare say somewhat blinking and near-sighted.

THERESA. Her eyes begin to fail a little, to be sure; but she's so much afraid of being thought old, that she never wears spectacles in company.

PHELIM. (*aside*) So much the better for brave Phelim O'Flinn— (*aloud*) Do you think, my dear, that if the Captain was to come down unexpectedly, Miss Laura would marry him at once, off hand.—(*Theresa hesitates*)—I ask, my dear ma'am, only because I am terribly interested for my frind the Captain. 'Pon my honor and soul, (*with an air of importance*) ma'am, I know him and love him as well as myself.

SAWNY. (*who has been listening attentively—aside*) Wha' does the loon mean by a' these questions?

THERESA. (*aside*) Perhaps this is some confidential friend, sent by the Captain to know how the land lies. (*To Phelim*)—Are you really, sir, a true friend to Captain O'Brien?

PHELIM. (*with great earnestness*) I am, good lady; by all the immortal powers of love; by the blessed vartue of my Captain's commission—Poh! what am I after saying?—I mean by—by every thing that's beautiful under the sun—by your own sweet self—I am; in troth, I am.

THERESA. Why, then, sir, I do believe that if the Captain were to come here now he might marry Laura without delay. She has strong reasons for wishing to be out of the power of her guardian as soon as possible.

PHELIM. (*aside*) Every thing as I could wish it—Now or never, Phelim—(*to Theresa*) My dear, I've just taken a great longing for a few glasses of wine. Let me have a bottle.

THERESA. The friend of Captain O'Brien shall have what he desires in an instant.

[*Exit.*

SAWNY. Wha the deil are ye aboot, mon? Why did ye ca' for wine, when ye like what ye like what ye hae before ye better?

PHELIM. Just to drive away the stink of the whiskey. Be aisy—my fortune's made, and so is yours, if you know how to behave yourself. You shall have the old one, the furnished house and the doubloons, and I'll marry Miss Laura and the 100,000 dollars.

SAWNY. Why, laddie, hae ye lost your senses?

PHELIM. Didn't you hear that long talk between ould madam and myself? The young lady has a fortune of a hundred thousand dollars; she is ready to marry this Captain O'Brien in a minute, tho' she never saw him but once; and I am as like the captain as two eggs. Didn't you mind how she described him? Just, as if any one had sint her a letter to draw my picture from. Mind now and look at *me*. Tall—well-built—of a good ginteel shape—handsome—pretty behaved, with great dale of agree-able gab—merry—jovial—a tight hand at a song, and the devil among the girls. Why, by the powers, if I was made exactly after him, I couldn't be a greater model of him nor I am. Remember now, Sawny, from this minute I'm Captain O'Brien in disguise—do you take me?

SAWNY. Wha the deil will believe ye, do ye think?

PHELIM. Every one, Sawny. Love, like liquor, disguises the best of us at times. My love was so headstrong and impatient, (I'm Captain O'Brien, recollect) that I couldn't wait for the snail-marching of the troops—Got lave of absence; doused my regimentals; put on a brown coat, (to be sure, it would be better if it wasn't quite so ould and threadbare) took horse, and gallop'd down the river, like the Podereen Mare! Then I came here, still disguised, to sound the ould mother duenna[21]—and the instant I got out of her the secret that my own sweet Laura loves me, I tell the whole truth of who I am; tho', by my soul, that same truth will lie a great big lie—get introduced to the

21. Spanish for governess or chaperone.

dear cratur; sind for the priest, and consummate the business as fast as possible.

SAWNY. But hae ye thought of the consequence of being detected?

PHELIM. Consequence? Not I.

SAWNY. Do ye ken that ye are not now in the United States? Na public trial—na fair and open exanimation of witnesses; na fixed, impartial laws; na jury—

PHELIM. And no lawyers, I dare say, to bother the witnesses! But sure, the barbarians couldn't hurt a poor fellow for the like of this? Oh, no fear of it. If we succeed, we're made for ever! If not, it will be only a bit of a joke—a little Irish humbug, carried on just for diversion.

SAWNY. And hae ye the conscience to deceive a young lassie in sic a way? It is na just, Phelim.

PHELIM. Won't I make her as good a husband as the best of their captains—aye, or their ginirals either. She shall have kindness and kissing galore, and a full share of every dollar of her fortune, as long as there is a farthing of it left.

SAWNY. I dunna like the scheme at a'—It's vary dishonest, and the profit of it vary uncertain.

PHELIM. Come, Sawny, you shall have ten thousand out of the hundred thousand dollars that I'm to get—and then you know all the folks will be *booing* and *booing* to you, as if you were a *laird*.

SAWNY. (*aside*) Gude troth, that alters the case—(*aloud*) I know, Phelim, you're a brae, generous cheel; but hoo can I tell, laddie, that ye winna wrong me oot o' the ten thousand dollars, sin ye are sae ready to cheat this young lassie oot o' ten times the sum?

PHELIM. I'd have you to know, Mr. Sawny, that the word of Phelim O'Flinn is as good as his bond—

SAWNY. (*aside*) Gin it is na better, it is na worth a bawbee.

PHELIM. But if you doubt it, honey, pull out your pin and ink, and be hanged to you, and I'll give you my note for the money, down upon the nail, payable on demand.

SAWNY. (*aside*) I mun tickle the fule's vanity, and then I'll hae a better chance of getting the siller—(*aloud*) No, Maister Phelim, I'd scorn to doubt ye; I'll tak your bare word.

PHELIM. Give us your paw, Sawny. Now you shall really get the cash; for you've touch'd myself on a tinder point——my honor. But if you had taken note or bond, you must have run your chance along with the rest of my creditors; and then, you know, devil a rap of the money ever you'd finger.

SAWNY. (*aside*) I know that vary weel.

PHELIM. Now, mind me, this story, (and a great story it will be, sure enough) of my coming here in disguise, will look better to be told by you nor myself—so, when the ould house-keeper returns, pritend a mighty great regard for her—whisper in her ear, that you are big with a terrible secret, and then let it all out, not forgetting a single word of what I tould you.

SAWNY. To oblige ye, Phelim, I'll do it.

PHELIM. If you like, I'll say you are some great jontleman in disguise, as well as myself.

SAWNY. Thank ye, mon; but I'd rather ye'd say I'm a vary honest, just, conscientious, cheap-selling travelling merchant, and mak them buy my goods without examining them too closely.

PHELIM. Aye, you blackguard! you must have large interest for your lies as well as your money. For the one you are to tell for me, you have the conscience to ask me to tell half a dozen for yourself. But now you talk of your goods, Sawny, let's see them—I'll be a good customer to you, myself. Come, open your pack,

and let me have some of your rings, and such like articles, as
a jontleman, the likes of myself, ought to wear. Quick! Don't
be stingy. Open your heart, or you may as well keep your pack
shut—Remember the ten thousand dollars.

SAWNY. Dunna tak mare than's absolutely necessary, tul the business
is feenallv settled—we dunna ken what ma happen.

*(Phelim takes several articles out of the pack,
all of which Sawny reluctantly parts with.)*

PHELIM. (*taking a watch-chain*) This watch will complately equip
me.

SAWNY. Haud your hond, mon! that article is na fit for a captain.
Though I ca' it gold to strangers, I winna deceive a friend—it's
only gilt.

PHELIM. No matter. It will look like gold as long as I shall condescend to wear it. (*Sawny angrily shuts up his pack*) I hear the
ould one coming.—Now, Sawny, my dear, remember all I tould
you, and the ten thousand dollars to boot.

Re-enter THERESA.

THERESA. Here, sir, is a glass of very nice Madeira. We'll drink
Captain O'Brien's good health.

PHELIM. (*with an affected and ridiculous air*) 'Pon my honor, my
dear lady, I'll drink it with all my heart; for it's all one as my
own—Ogh! I main it's my own best frind's! (*walks about and
nods to Sawny.*)

SAWNY. (*aside to Theresa*) Gude lady, I cou'd tell ye a vary great secret, gin I lik'd; and troth I love you so muckle that I'm almost
tempted to do it, though I promised hard to haud my tongue.

THERESA. My good sir, I never could keep another person's secrets
in my life. I'll sing you a little song about secrets.

SONG—THERESA.

When to banquets or weddings my neighbors invite me,
    To go there I seldom refuse, sir;
For good cheer and good chat do at all times delight me,
    As well as to hear what's the news, sir.

Then each dame who meets me, most civilly greets me,
    And exchanges her secrets for mine, sir.
So, like birds of a feather, we cluster together,
    And enliven discourse with good wine, sir,

A woman, they tell you, no secrets can keep,
    But i'faith that is all a humbug, sir;
The secrets of others she never let's sleep,
    But her own in her bosom lie snug, sir.

Then let each man his own secrets keep to himself,
    And not trust them with even his brother;
For if to divulge them he's such a weak elf,
    What the de'il can he expect from another?

SAWNY. Vary gude advice! But the secret I hae to tell concerns the young lassie we were talking of—Miss Laura.

THERESA. Oh, then, let me hear it by all means.

(Sawny and Theresa converse apart—
Phelim struts about the stage, rattling watch-chain, &c.)

THERESA. Bless me, say you so? Captain O'Brien in disguise! I thought there was something extraordinary about him!

SAWNY. Gude troth, he has assurance enough for a general.

THERESA. Captain O'Brien, I am rejoiced you are come!

PHELIM. What! Has that confounded rascal divulged ray secret? Oh, you villain!—Oh, you desaiver! (*Goes as if to beat Sawny.*)

THERESA. Dear good Captain, what he did was only to serve you.

PHELIM. (*aside*) And himself at the same time.

THERESA. Indeed, Captain, you must forgive him.

PHELIM. Well, my dear, I will, but it's only on your account; for, in troth and upon my honor, myself's ashamed to appear before my sweet Miss Laura in this disguisement.

THERESA. Oh, sir, don't let it trouble you. Love produces stranger things than these. I heard the judge's lady say that it once caused Jupiter,[22] the sovereign of the gods, to make himself a bull.

PHELIM. By the powers, it has caused myself to make a hundred bulls before now. But come now and introduce me to this young lady directly. I can wait no longer. I have waited, by my soul, too long already. But sure it was only to know whether the pretty lass was fond of me or not.

THERESA. Ah, you have stole that secret from me indeed. But, let's see—We must endeavor to conceal your arrival from the judge and his lady.

PHELIM. By my honor and soul, I wish it could be concealed from every one but Laura and the priest. I don't like to be seen even by myself in this mean disguise till the marriage is over.

THERESA. Deuce take it, here she comes! How unfortunate!

Enter SENORA DE LA PLATA.

SENORA DE LA PLATA. Theresa, 1 want you to pack up some of Don Bertoldo's trunks.

---

22. In Roman mythology, Jupiter was the king of the gods (known as Zeus to the Greeks).

PHELIM. (*aside*) Now or never! here goes—(*aloud*) Captain O'Brien, madam, has the very great honor of asking your lady-ship how d'ye do? I was so eager to set my eyes once more on Miss Laura, that I couldn't wait for my brother officers and the brave army under our command, but slipt on the first brown coat that was uppermost in my trunk, took horse and gallop'd down the river as if the devil drove me. How is my little jewel of a girl. Ogh! tho' I never saw her but once, to be sure her sweet image isn't painted on my heart in letters of brass.

SENORA DE LA PLATA. (*viewing Phelim with astonishment—aside*) What can the fellow mean?

PHELIM. (*aside*) She's near sighted sure enough—so much the better. (*aloud*) I beg your pardon, my dear, for not asking more about yourself. But my love for Miss Laura is so strong, it leath-ers every thing else out of my head—Why, you might as well stop the Missisippi, when in a fresh, with a pitch-fork.

SENORA DE LA PLATA. (*aside*) This fellow's impudence is amusing—For curiosity I'll suffer him to proceed.

PHELIM. (*aside*) She has doubts, I'm afraid!—(*aloud*) To be plain, my dear lady, the fury of my affection will put up with no de-lay. My poor heart is now blazing away with love, all as one as a still of whisky on fire. So, if you'll just bring me to Miss Laura, she shall be, with the assistance of the priest, this day a wife—and this day nine months—but no matter for that.

SENORA DE LA PLATA. (*aside*) His size and figure have some resem-blance to O'Brien—and she has seen *him* but once.

PHELIM. Come, my dear jewel! don't be after boggling so much about the matter.

SAWNY. (*aside to Phelim*) Dinna speak so lood mon! Boo and be re-spectful to the lady, or I wad na gie ye a bawbee for your chance.

(*Phelim and Sawny converse apart at the back of the stage—Phelim opens and rummages Sawny's pack.*)

SENORA DE LA PLATA. (*aside*) If it were possible to make this man impose upon Laura, it would be far better than sending her to the Havanna—O'Brien might possibly follow her there—But if I could make her marry this impostor, she would be for ever out of O'Brien's reach. His love for her would be converted into pity or scorn, and I should then reign without a rival over his heart as well as his understanding. Some tutoring may do a great deal with this forward fellow—I'll try, at all events—If the imposture is found out, I can only pretend to have been deceived myself.

PHELIM. (*lugs forward Sawny's pack*) Come, you sir, let me see all your fine affairs, that I may make handsome presents to the ladies. What's the price of this? (*taking a locket*)

SAWNY. Twa hundred dollars.

PHELIM. And of this? (*taking another article*)

SAWNY. One hundred dollars.

PHELIM. Give me lave, madam—(*presents the first to Senora de la Plata*) And do you, my dear, (*to Theresa*) take this.

SAWNY. (*aside to Phelim, in great anger*) Oons, mon, what are ye aboot! ye hae geen awa what cost me twenty good hard dollars. Ye shall get na mare frae me. Be as generous as ye like with ony one's property but Sawny M'Gregor's. (*shuts up the pack*)

PHELIM. (*aside to Sawny*) Oh, you mean spalpeen!

SENORA DE LA PLATA. (*looking more closely at Phelim*) Captain O'Brien I have to ask you a thousand pardons. I really did not know you at first. Your complexion is somewhat altered since I had the pleasure of seeing you at Monsieur Bordell's.

PHELIM. My dear lady, I've had a severe fit of the fever and ague lately; and that, you know, always affects a man's colour. I am not quite recovered of it yet, though I had the very best doctors to attind me. By my honor, ma'am, there's no doctors in the world to be compared with our's in the United States. They'll try half a dozen ways at the same time of curing a man, and they change them all every now and then, just for experiment; so that their patients shan't have to say they don't get variety at least for their money.

SENORA DE LA PLATA. Excellent!—When did you see our friend Monsieur Bordell's family?

PHELIM. A few days ago, madam. They are all brave and hearty, and desired to be remembered to you.

SENORA DE LA PLATA. His children were quite recovered, I hope.

PHELIM. All of them, my lady—sweet little girls, to be sure they are.

SENORA DE LA PLATA. (*whispering Phelim*) You forget,—Captain— they are all boys.

PHELIM. Burn my stupid head, so they are. The girls are all boys. This fever and ague plays the mischief with a man's memory as well as his complexion.

SENORA DE LA PLATA. Permit me, captain, to conduct you to the saloon, and we shall converse on the subject of your marriage with Donna Laura.

PHELIM. With all my heart—(*aside*) I'm a made man.

SENORA DE LA PLATA. Go, Theresa, and announce the arrival of Captain O'Brien to my lovely Laura. Tell her I shall have the pleasure of introducing him to her in less than an hour.

[*Exit, Theresa.*

PHELIM. Do you, Mr. M'Gregor, go and see if my rascally servants are coming with my horses and my baggage.

SAWNY. (*aside*) Your baggage! Isn't a' upon your back?

PHELIM. (*aside to Sawny*) Why, you booby, have you no gumption?

SAWNY. (*aside*) Oh! I ken what you're aboot—(*aloud*) Yes, an' please
your honor, I'll search for them directly, though I'm afraid they
winna be here to-day—(*aside to Phelim*) Tak gude heed now,
Phelim, and be vary cautious to let nathing slip that may betray
the grog-shop. Boo and be respectful to every body.

[*Exit.*

PHELIM. I have a pair of as great whiskey-drinking, idle rascals of
servants, madam, as any in America. They lost me, about a week
since, a fine racehorse I imported myself from Dublin, that
won the king's plate[23] five years successfully on the Curragh of
Kildare. I wouldn't be the least surprised now if they got drunk
and run away with my fine cattle, my brace of hair-trigger pis-
tols, my military cloak and a pair of elegant portmanteaus.

SENORA DE LA PLATA. Please to follow me, captain.

PHELIM. (*aside*) Well, what it is to have a dashing spirit, that's neither ashamed nor afraid of any thing.

[*Exeunt.*

23. A traditional British horseracing trophy.

ACT III.
SCENE—A Library.

LAURA—THERESA.

LAURA. What you tell me, Theresa, astonishes me much. I saw the two men you speak of as they entered the house, and neither of them I'm sure was Captain O'Brien?

THERESA. Is it possible?—Blessed Virgin! what motive can the impostor have for his wickedness?

LAURA. The questions he asked of you convince me that his only object is to obtain my fortune; yet, how to account for the conduct of Senora de la Plata. She did not address him by the name of O'Brien at first, you say?

THERESA. No, lady—she hesitated for some time; seemed deep in thought; and then, all at once, spoke to him as the Captain.

LAURA. It must be so—she is still intent on separating O'Brien and me for ever; and she supposes that this imposture affords her better means of effecting her purpose than any she has yet devised,

THERESA. What a roasting she'll get in purgatory for all this.

Enter a **SERVANT.**

SERVANT. (*to Laura*) A young woman, madam, requests to see you. She appears to be in great distress.

LAURA. Conduct her to me immediately.

[*Exit Servant.*

THERESA. Who can this be?

Enter LUCY MARGLAND.

LUCY, (*to Laura*) Madam, I entreat your pardon for troubling you. There is now in this house a man who has injured me cruelly.

THERESA. This very villain, I dare say. What is his name?

LUCY. Mr. Phelim O'Flinn. I became acquainted with him, unfortunately for me, as he was travelling through Tennessee for the Natchez. He pretended to love me, and I believed him—but too well.

THERESA. Poor girl! What did he do to you then?

LUCY. He deceived me—and I was undone!

THERESA. By St. Bridget,[24] purgatory is too good for him—(*aside*) I dare say the poor girl's with child.

LUCY. I left my family to avoid disgrace; for I found it could not much longer be concealed.—With the hope of prevailing on my seducer to repair by marriage the injury he had done me, I followed him to the Natchez; but when I arrived there, I learned he had just gone on for New-Orleans. I then got into the first boat that was passing down, and we happened to be opposite to this house when he and another man were going into it.

THERESA. Poor injured innocent!—How long since tins misfortune befel you?

LUCY. Between seven and eight months.

THERESA. So that in about six weeks you may be brought to bed. Mercy on us!

24. St. Bridget (also Brigid) was an Irish abbess venerated for her virginity.

LAURA. I pity you, sincerely. I should be happy if I could obtain for you the reparation you seek.

LUCY. Ah! madam, that I were worthy of offering you my thanks! (*weeps*)

LAURA. Be comforted; perhaps this gentleman may yet be just and kind to you.

THERESA. (*aside*) A bright thought has just come into my head.

LUCY. When I saw Mr. O'Flinn entering this house, I enquired who lived in it; and you, madam, were represented to me as the most amiable and compassionate of your sex. I hoped, (for the unfortunate will always hope) that if you would interest yourself for me, you might persuade Mr. O'Flinn to take pity on my sufferings.

LAURA. I wish it were in my power.

THERESA. Yes; I have it. She shall be an honest woman before she sleeps, as sure as I'm a maid. I tell you, Donna Laura, this young woman shall be a wife long before she's a mother—aye, a bride this very day, if you will assist in the scheme I have formed.

LAURA. What is it, Theresa? If it is proper, I'll cheerfully do any thing that is right to promote it.

THERESA. This wicked seducer wishes to impose himself on you as Captain O'Brien; and there is no doubt but my lady, the Senora, is an accomplice in his plot. Now then, when she introduces him to you, if you will only pretend that you believe him to be the real Captain O'Brien; receive his addresses, and agree to be privately married to him—

LAURA. Why, Theresa, have you lost your senses?

THERESA. No, no, sweet lady—I say, consent to a private marriage, on condition that you shall be veiled during the ceremony.

He'll make no objection, I am sure, as he is so eager to carry on his wicked deceit.

LAURA. And what then?

THERESA. Why then, my dear, I'll dress up this young woman to appear like you—put a veil over her face, and Mr. Phelim O'Flinn shall marry *her* instead of *you.*

LAURA. But would such a marriage be valid?

THERESA. It shall be made so, never fear. I'll send instantly for our worthy priest, Father Francisco, and acquaint him with the whole affair. He loves to do justice to the injured; and I'll warrant me he'll find a way of managing the business as we wish.

LUCY. Heaven bless you, madam!

LAURA. But, Theresa, can I with propriety consent to impose even upon this impostor?

THERESA. To be sure, my dear lady, when your object is to do good without hurting any one. The stratagem that confounds wickedness, and converts its own wiles into the means of doing justice, is fair and laudable. By this plan of mine, we shall disappoint the malignity of Senora de la Plata, and defeat the purpose of this base man; not by injuring him, but by making him repair the injury he has already done.

LAURA. Your reasons appear unanswerable.

THERESA. Aye marry, are they! We should all of us set our faces against these wretches of Irishmen. I tremble myself at the thought of them. Who can tell how soon poor Lucy's case may be one's own? But here comes my lady, with that wicked fellow. Let us retire and arrange our plan. Lucy must be concealed for the present—(*aside as they retire*) Oh, dear, how I do dread these Irishmen. The young Kentucky crackers are bad enough, but both together, Saint Bridget herself could hardly resist.

Enter SENORA DE LA PLATA *and* PHELIM O'FLINN.

SENORA DE LA PLATA. Now, Captain, remember what I have told you. The very short acquaintance you have had with Donna Laura, makes it requisite that you should attend to what I say, and act as I direct. I am very desirous that you and Laura should be immediately married, because I wish to see you both happy.

PHELIM. Indeed, my lady, I'm for ever obliged to you.

SENORA DE LA PLATA. Be careful to repress the uncouth boisterousness of your manner, and be not too forward or presuming. It is only by gentleness and a modest demeanor, that such a lady as Donna Laura can be won.

PHELIM. Ogh! if modesty would do, the business is as good as settled; for an't I an Irishman? But, plaise your ladyship, mayn't I give her a little kiss, just as much as to say, I'm glad to see you again, my jewel!

SENORA DE LA PLATA. By no means. Recollect that you have been only once in her company.

PHELIM. My dear, I've kissed young jontlewomen without even that same, before now. I suppose I mustn't even touch her?

SENORA DE LA PLATA. Only her hand, in a very delicate manner. In speaking to her, your voice must be lowered, and you must approach her with trembling diffidence!

PHELIM. (*aside*) Nothing could ever make myself tremble but a sheriff or a constable.

SENORA DE LA PLATA. Let your countenance express the ardent hopes of your soul; but mingled with anxiety, and chastened by apprehension. Your tongue should falter—your breathing be quickened—and in your eye there should glisten the tear of enraptured joy.

PHELIM. (*aside*) I never could cry cither, except when making it up with a friend, after fighting together, over a jug of punch.

SENORA DE LA PLATA. Observe now, and try to imitate me! When you first address Donna Laura, speak thus—"Lovely Laura! Sovereign of my heart! Divinity of my existence! Your angelic presence fills my soul with rapture, as the genial beams of Apollo impregnate the barren earth."

PHELIM. Lovely Miss Laura! Sovereign—No, as we're so soon to be a republic, president will do better—President of my own heart— without either congress, judge or jury to impeach or to bother you! Your angel of a face makes me pregnant with joy—Poh! begging your pardon, my dear, wouldn't that be fitter for *her* to say to *me*? Sure a man can't be made pregnant with any thing.

SENORA DE LA PLATA. Well, Captain, say what you please yourself. I shall bring Laura to you immediately.

[*Exit.*

PHELIM. (*solus*) Hasn't she a great dale of assurance to be after larning Phelim O'Flinn how to make love? I that come from the land of love-making! I that have sarved two apprenticeships to the business already, since I first set up in it for myself! I must not lay my hand on her—no, nor give her a single kiss! I believe they're afraid the soft cratur's made of touchwood.

Enter SENORA DE LA PLATA *and* LAURA.

SENORA DE LA PLATA. Here, my dear child, is the Captain. I know his arrival will delight you.

PHELIM. (*affecting bashfulness and apprehension*) How do you do, Mademoiselle Laura? It's so long since I've seen you, tho' I know you again as well as if it was only yesterday. To be sure this same love doesn't furbish up a man's memory.

SENORA DE LA PLATA. (*aside to Pheim*) Call her Senora! That's the mode of addressing a Spanish lady.

PHELIM. (to Laura) Senora Laura, I main—I've almost forgot all my Spanish, since I took to speaking French so much of late.

LAURA. I hope, Captain, you have been well.

PHELIM. (*aside*) Phelim for ever! It will soon be Phelim O'Flinn, *Esquire.*

SENORA DE LA PLATA. (*aside*) Poor fool How easy these children are deceived—O'Brien is safe!

PHELIM. Please your ladyship, Senora Laura, I've not been very well, tho' I thank you all the same as if I hadn't that cursed fit of the fever and ague at the Natchez. It has altered my looks, aye, and my spaking a great dale, I'm told, Senora Laura.

LAURA. (*aside*) Impudent impostor. (*aloud*) Sir, I perceive the alteration very plainly.

PHELIM. But sure the like of that can make no alteration in a body's affections.

(Laura curtsies.)

SENORA DE LA PLATA. Let me now speak to you both, without ceremony. Your affection for each other has been known to me some time. I know too that Don Bertoldo will never consent to your marriage—

PHELIM. Devil fire the ould rogue!—What objection can he or any one else have to Phelim—ogh! to Captain O'Brien?

SENORA DE LA PLATA. For purposes, I fear, the most unworthy and perfidious, with respect to your honor, my Laura, he intends to take you with him to the Havanna, and thence to Spain; where, if you refuse to act as he desires, he may, by his authority as your guardian, shut you up in a convent as long as you live.

PHELIM. Oh, the thief! Wouldn't that be worse nor murder? Burying one sweet cratur alive, and preventing so many others from being born.

SENORA DE LA PLATA. The only way to secure your happiness, my love, is by an immediate private marriage with Captain O'Brien.

LAURA. (*aside*) Treacherous hypocrite!

SENORA DE LA PLATA. I shall now leave you by yourselves. Your felicity depends on your following my advice.—(*aside to Phelim*) Now, if you do not succeed, it is your own fault—(*to Laura*) Take care, my dear, that Don Bertoldo shall not know of the Captain's arrival—he would immediately defeat your hopes.

[*Exit.*

LAURA *and* PHELIM.

PHELIM. (*aside*) Now, how must I begin?

LAURA. (*aside*) What unparalleled assurance! I'll try, for curiosity, if it is possible to confound or abash his impudence.

PHELIM. Senora Laura, your divinity of an angel face gives me more pleasure than all the earth; aye, or than the sea, if it was turned into punch!—Oh, now, if your heart is pregnant with joy, we'll soon put our finger in the eye of this vile ould fellow, that wants to take you away from my longing arms.—(*aside*) She doesn't spake; but that's only modesty I suppose—(*aloud*) So now, my sweet Senora Laura, if you'll only let me sind for the priest of the parish, every thing shall be settled this very night. Spake to me, my jewel of a Senora!

LAURA. Your arrival so soon, sir, has surprised me.

PHELIM. By my soul, it surprises myself; but Phelim—ogh! Captain O'Brien! likes to give an agreeable surprise to any one he loves. If it wasn't for that, I'd have wrote to you to tell you I was coming. But, in troth, I'm not very fond of writing—a body can spake more to the purpose with his tongue in five minutes, nor with his pin in an hour.

LAURA. You forget, sir—here is a letter of your's, written only a few days ago, in which you informed me that you feared you could not be here before this evening or to-morrow morning. (*shows a letter*)

PHELIM. (*aside*) By the powers, I'm bogg'd!——What will you do now, Phelim?—(*takes the letter and examines it—aloud*) Oh! murder! murder! What will the impudence of mankind come to at last!—A forgery, Senora!—A forgery, by St. Patrick, and all the saints, male and female, on the face of the earth—committed by some son of a ......; begging your pardon, Senora— by some rascal invious of my happiness. Oh! isn't it the devil to attempt for to take away my sweet character, in such a base, cowardly way. I'd sooner a man would come and give me a pair of black eyes behind my back. This fellow wants to make you believe that he is me; but it's I that's—eh! aye, I that's—my-self—the real Captain O'Brien. Sure no one would be such a fool as to change himself when he was going a-courting.

LAURA. (*aside*) Nothing can confound his assurance—(*aloud*) You recollect, sir, the picture I gave you. I wish to see it, if you have it with you.

PHELIM. (*aside*) She's not so bashful either, if she gives a man a present at first sight—(*aloud*) Oh! yes, Senora; that beautiful picture of your's—to be sure I didn't hug it close to my heart, as long as I had it.

LAURA. Have you then lost it, sir?

PHELIM. Wait, and I'll tell you. I didn't lose it, though it was taken from me—but, by the powers, it cost the fellow that has it and fifteen more of his comrades, their lives. I went out, Senora, and marched a small party of troops against the Indians—

LAURA. I thought you were at peace with them.

PHELIM. Oh, my dear, didn't you hear of an immense gang of
them that earns their living by plundering the people between
Tennessee and the Natchez. There's about two hundred of the
villains. I marched out with a little party of about twenty men
under my command. We attacked them with great bravery—
myself was foremost—and, after spitting about fifteen of them
on my own sword, as nately as if they were put down to roast,
I was overpowered, and the cruel thieves tore away the picture
from my aching heart!—If it was an honest poor white man that
robb'd me of it, I wouldn't think half so much about it; but the
idea that you may be at this moment hanging round the neck,
or dangling out of the nostrils of a blackguard, red rascal, makes
myself as melancholy as the devil—(*pretends to weep*)—In troth,
I grieved a vast dale more about that same picture, than for all
the money they took from me at the same time, and sure enough
that was no trifle. Faith, it was the biggest half of the last gale of
rint I received from my Connaught estate. Bad luck to that same
estate—I am always losing by it. The whole of the half year's rint
before that was sint by my agent, ould Larry Malowney, to Pat
Flannigan, a merchant in Charleston. As soon as Pat gets the
money into his hands, what does he do but turn bankrupt for
the binifit of his creditors—and when all came to all, he was just
able to pay them—nothing in the pound.

LAURA. I thought, sir, you told me you had no fortune whatever!

PHELIM. Faith and that wasn't the first lie my modesty has made me
tell. I felt unaisy, for fear you might fall in love with my dirty
acres instead of my sweet self; but now, since I know you love
me, I may let the secret out. I never could bear the idea of marrying for money. In troth, I can't tell whether you have got any
or -not. If I thought you were rich, I couldn't be half so fond
of you as I am, do my best. The devil a thing I want, my dear
Senora, but your own bare self.

LAURA. Pray, sir, did you hear any thing further of that man who
you told me behaved so ill at the Natchez?

PHELIM. Do you recollect his name?

LAURA. I think it was one Phelim O'Flinn.

PHELIM. (*aside—starts*) Devil burn me, am I after abusing my-self?—(*aloud*) Phelim O'Flinn? aye, I remember him—He kept a bit of a grog-shop at the Natchez. I heard nothing about him more nor what I told you. I never keep company with such low main blackguards.

LAURA. (*aside*) Diverting impudence!

PHELIM. But, my dear jewel of a Senora, don't forget what my lady said to us—Do now let me sind for the priest.

LAURA. I am afraid, sir, I cannot refuse you.

PHELIM. (*aside*) I knew you couldn't. It's Phelim O'Flinn, *Esquire*, sure enough. (*to her*) Thank you, my jewel! (*going to take her in his arms—she recedes*) Sure now you'll let me take a few little kisses off your sweet lips—It's always the custom in my coun-try, whenever we make a bargain, to get earnest.

LAURA. (*retiring*) That is a liberty, sir, which I cannot allow.

PHELIM. Oh, I ask your pardon, my dear. Myself thought that when a young lady liked a lad well enough to consint to marry him, she would be no ways unaisy at giving him a kiss.

LAURA. You have no doubt, sir, brought your commission with you? The notary who makes the marriage contract may re-quire to see it.

PHELIM. (*aside*) Bogged again!—(*aloud, after rummaging his pockets*) Oh, my stupid head. Didn't the Indian thieves take it from me as well as the picture and the money. I put it in my pocket when I marched to the battle, for fear the blackguards might refuse me my parole of honor if I was taken prisoner. When they got hold of the commission, I says to the thief that held it, devil fire you, my dear, give me back that bit of paper—What use can it be of to you, says he—Who knows, says another, but there's some witchcraft in it—May be, says a third, it was the devil himself that scratched all these pot-hooks and hangers; for the blockheads, you know, never get any larning; but for all I could do or say they wouldn't give it to me. So when I returned to the Natchez, I was obliged to send away an express to the City of Washington with my positive orders to the President to make me out another commission immediately, and not to delay at his peril—and, by my soul, it will be worse for him, if he doesn't mind what I said.

LAURA. Perhaps your commission will not he required. Good morning, sir; I shall send Theresa to inform you how the marriage ceremony is to take place.

PHELIM. (*going towards her and stretching forth his arms—she retires, curtsying and exit*) Just one little kiss now! You'd rather have it, for all that—Myself doesn't like people giving themselves such airs. Phelim O'Flinn has kiss'd many a handsomer girl. I wish Sawny was here now that I might tell him my good luck. I'll make that same Sawny my steward—He'll let no one chate me but himself, and one rogue in a family is better than a dozen. Then he'll force every one to pay what they owe me, or go to law with them. This same law is not so bad a thing either, when a man gets rich. To be sure, they say it's open to the poor as well as the rich; aye, faith, just like the New-York hotel, where a poor man will get very good tratement, if he has only plenty of money to spind. The law is a mighty good sort of a thing for a man to follow, but the devil when it follows him. Some rogues follow it; others are followed by it—but the last have the worst of the bargain. Well, when I get rich, I'll turn very honest all at once, and pay off all my debts. Eh! Phelim, will that be right? No, by my soul, it would be a piece of barbarous cruelty to a great many worthy jontlemen that live so genteel and so splendid, honest souls, without ever paying any debt at all— Wouldn't the world point at them and abuse them, if I was to put it into their heads by paying my debts? Then, to be sure, I won't pay a visit to the land of potatoes and drive away in a fine coach—Death and ouns! how Judy Magragh will stare when she sees me in it—Devil relieve her; why didn't she marry me when I asked her seven years ago? Then there's Father Farrell, that larned me my letters before I was fifteen years ould—he shall get share of many a good jug of punch for his pains; but as for that blackguard of a jontleman, the consaited guager, I'll not know him again—but, by my soul, I'll give him a little taste of shillelah for ould acquaintance sake. But won't the real Captain O'Brien, when he comes on, make a terrible rout about all this? Who cares? Can't I shoot him if he likes—He'll say no more after that: and it will clear my character as well as my conscience. Stop now, Phelim. If I pritend to be Captain O'Brien, and not Phelim O'Flinn, will the marriage stand good in law, so that I may finger the cash? (*muses*) Confound this same law, it's always in my way, baulking or bothering me! But I dare say the priest could manage the matter. I must try to coax him. It would be the devil to be disappointed after going on well so far. The ould judge would make nothing, curse on his conscience, of chateing me out of my fortune, if he could.

Enter THERESA.

THERESA. Captain, I have sent for the priest, and expect him in a few minutes. Will you remain here till he comes, and amuse yourself with some of those books?

PHELIM. I have so much larning already, my dear, that reading is of no use to me; so, if it's all one to you, I'd rather go back to your room, and wash down another plate of the savoury stew with the remainder of the Madeira.

THERESA. Come along then—(*aside*) Tho' I protest I'm almost afraid to trust myself with such a wicked seducer. Who knows what he may do?

[*Exeunt.*

ACT IV.

SCENE—Theresa's Apartment.

PHELIM. (*seated at a table—wine, &c. before him*) Now, I think, I may do. This is the way I'll soon fare, from morning to night, and every day in the week will be Sunday to me.

Enter THERESA *and* FATHER FRANCISCO.

THERESA. This, sir, is Father Francisco, our worthy priest. I have already told him what we wish to have done; and explained to him *very fully*, I assure you, why both you and Donna Laura are desirous that the ceremony should be performed immediately in a private manner.

PHELIM. (*shakes the priest by the hand*) How are you, honey? The very sight of your cloth is my delight. Devil burn the better Roman Catholic in your whole community nor Phe—Capt. O'Brien.

FATHER FRANCISCO. (*aside*) Impudent villain!—(*to Phelim*) So, sir, you intend entering into the happy state of wedlock.

PHELIM. Yes, holy father, with your lave; for, upon my conscience, I am so good a Catholic that I never vinture upon doing any thing without first asking the advice of a priest.

THERESA. My young lady has directed me to tell you, Captain, that she wishes no one to be present at the marriage ceremony but Father Francisco and myself. She desires also to be veiled during the performance of it. She is very young, you know, and this is a very terrible business. I'm sure, though I'm a few years older myself, I should not be able to show my face while the priest was at work on such an occasion.

PHELIM. Myself doesn't care what Senora Laura wears! If she hadn't a stitch on her back, she'd be mighty well dressed to suit me.

THERESA. I must now attend her. As soon as she is ready I'll come and inform you—(*aside*) We'll soon make poor Lucy an honest woman. I hope I may have some one to do as much for me, if ever any of the crackers or the Irishmen should make it necessary.

[*Exit.*

PHELIM *and* FATHER FRANCISCO.

PHELIM. I was just telling you, father, how good a Catholic I am.

FATHER FRANCISCO. Sir, I am always glad to find men who venerate our holy religion. He who sincerely believes its sacred principles and obeys its precepts will never fail to act uprightly.

PHELIM. Never, Father.

FATHER FRANCISCO. To speak with truth—

PHELIM. Very right, by my soul.

FATHER FRANCISCO. And to shun every species of fraud, deceitfulness and imposture.

PHELIM. (*appearing confused and uneasy*) Yes, yes, father, yes. Now, Father Francisco, you may believe me, I have always had the devil's own liking for a priest. In the town where I was born, there was a brace of them, mighty honest pretty behaved souls; and to be sure I didn't take great notice of them both. May be you have heard of them—Father Farrell, the friar, and Father Donnelan, the priest of the parish of Mullakilty?

FATHER FRANCISCO. Never before, sir.

PHELIM. Never a quarter of a year passed over my head, that I didn't sind each of them a small present of half a score sacks of wheat, as many of oats and potatoes, a fat sheep, and a side of beef to put in salt; with now and then a few little young pigs to make black-puddings out of. Then I never went to dinner when I had any thing very nice to eat, that they wern't both invited to the big house. Paddy Donnelan, poor soul, soon grew so fat that he wasn't able to ride to mass conveniently, and so I sint to Dublin for a little noddy for him to put his ould bones in, not forgetting a snug lump of a horse to draw it, that I gave my neighbor, Bob Flaherty, five-and-twenty golden guineas for.

FATHER FRANCISCO. Very generous, indeed.

PHELIM. The women, I dare say, tould you what a pretty estate was left me in Connaught by my ould uncle, Taydy O'Brien?

FATHER FRANCISCO. Not a word.

PHELIM. To be sure it never did me much good; for what with giving away in charity, and making prisents to the priests and the church, myself was often bogged up to the ears in debt—Tho' I could always find enough to do, as every good Catholic ought, by jontlemen of your cloth—But now that I'm going to marry this great fortune of a hundred thousand dollars, I'll be able to do the thing, (do you mind Father) more genteely nor ever. I hope, Father, your're not too hard upon a body at confession?

FATHER FRANCISCO. We cannot, sir, you know, give any absolution unless to sincere repentance be added the utmost possible reparation for injuries committed. Is there any thing for which you stand in need of forgiveness? If the recollection of some heavy misconduct afflicts your conscience, you had better immediately confess it, and make every atonement in your power for any wrong you may have done.

PHELIM. (*pausing*) Eh! (*aside*) By my soul I'd better let it alone till the marriage is over. It would be the devil to do pinnance for a thing without having the binifit of it secured first—(*aloud*) Oh, no, Father, I was only thinking of a few wild tricks, such as all of us play when we are young. In troth my conscience was always mighty tinder. These little foibles began to make it unaisy. I have one thing of consequence, however, to say to you.

FATHER FRANCISCO. What is it?

PHELIM. I suppose I needn't tell you that this judge, Don Bertoldo, is a great rogue; a devil of a canat, as we call it. He'd think no more of chateing a man, than you or I would of going to mass, or blessing ourselves.

FATHER FRANCISCO. Well, sir!

PHELIM. He knows nothing at all about this marriage. Now, if he could find out any cursed lawyer's quibble, any knaving pretence to object to it, and overturn it, the ould thief would be after robbing me of my fine fortune, that I'll do so much good with to the church. (*significantly*)

FATHER FRANCISCO. Be under no apprehensions. Let me know your Christian name, and I'll engage that your marriage shall be completely binding.

PHELIM. My Christian name, and please your reverence, is Phelim.

FATHER FRANCISCO. Enough.

PHELIM. (*shakes hands with him*) Good luck to you, honey. May you have every day of your life, a christening breakfast, a burial for dinner, and a wedding supper, to cheer your heart.

Enter **THERESA.**

THERESA. Captain, the bride is now ready. I come to conduct you to her apartment; but we must go by a circuitous way, round the piazza, lest Don Bertoldo should meet us as he passes to the hall, where he is now going to hold an audience.

PHELIM. An audience! What's that, my dear?

FATHER FRANCISCO. What you would call a court of justice.

PHELIM. Take me as far out of the way of it as you choose—(*aside*) I never had any great liking for such places—(*aloud*) So go on— Wherever you lead me I'm ready to follow, first or last.

[*Exeunt.*

SCENE—The Hall of Audience.

DON BERTOLDO, *the* SCRIVANO,[25] ALGUAZILS, *&c.—Books, Papers, &c.—The Judge is seated at the top of the table, the Scrivano at the bottom of it.*

DON BERTOLDO. Alguazils, you may retire till you are called—(*they go*)—This, Senor Scrivano, is the last audience I shall hold in Louisiana. I hope it will not be an unprofitable one—(*pulls out an empty money-bag, and shakes it*)

SCRIVANO. No fear of that, Senor—Many of your worship's suitors supposing that your decisions will be considered binding by the American tribunals, are urgent to obtain your decrees in their favor.

DON BERTOLDO. It is on that account that I have determined to give judgments this day in favor of every suitor who applies to me in a *proper manner.*

SCRIVANO. Your worship is always right; there would be no use now in postponing a suit—no more fees or presents can be expected after to-day.

DON BERTOLDO. No more, indeed—Curse this treaty of cession. But come, let me know which cause stands first for my consideration.

SCRIVANO. (*examines papers*) That between the heirs of Dan Manuel Peralta, which has been depending for twenty-one years and seven—

DON BERTOLDO. Nonsense! There are scores of such causes. I want not the oldest but the best—the best, I mean, in the fee-book. It is that alone which establishes the point of precedency between my suitors.

25. A clerk.

SCRIVANO. I ask pardon, Senor; I forgot. One of the *best* causes then, I think, is that which is founded on the memorial of Don Antonio Gaspar, against Don Felix Pereira, demanding to be put into possession of the plantation, consisting of one thousand acres, left him by his father; which Don Felix has, without any pretence or title, seized and occupied for five years past. It appears, from the defendant's own declaration, that he has no right whatever to the property in dispute.

DON BERTOLDO. Right! Senor Scrivano! right!—Don't use such language to me. One of the cursed Americans could do no more.

SCRIVANO. Forgive me.

DON BERTOLDO. Tell me not of right; but tell me how much the parties have already given. Let us examine. (*they examine a memorandum-book*)

SCRIVANO. It appears. Senor, that Don Felix has already given, at different times, one thousand dollars to prolong the suit.

DON BERTOLDO. And he has no reason to complain. He has had five crops from the land.

SCRIVANO. Indeed, Senor, it would have been scandalous injustice to have let him pay so much money for nothing; but it also appears that Don Gaspar has since given exactly the same sum. How then, Senor, shall I make out your final decree? Shall I read any of the documents?

DON BERTOLDO. Damn the documents! my fee-book, is all the proof I want. Let me see—the parties have given equally, then I decree that the plantation be equally divided between them.

SCRIVANO. Nothing can be fairer.

Enter a **SERVANT.**

SERVANT. Don Antonio Gaspar requests permission to speak with your worship.

DON BERTOLDO. Shew him in. [*Exit Servant.*] Delay drawing up the decree, perhaps Don Antonio may furnish us with some further proofs.

Enter **DON ANTONIO.**

DON ANTONIO. I come, Senor, to entreat your decree that Don Felix shall give up the plantation he has so long and unjustly withheld from me. I presume to be thus urgent, as it is supposed the American courts of law will consider your judgements to be final and decisive.

DON BERTOLDO. The supposition is just. Those tribunals will not have the insolent folly to set aside such wise and honest decisions as we always give. It is therefore that I have just ordered the Scrivano to draw up the final decree in yours as well as several other suits.

DON ANTONIO. I most humbly thank your worship. Indeed, my family has been reduced to extreme distress, from the length of time to which Don Felix has prolonged the proceedings.

(The Judge nods significantly to the Scrivano,
who whispers to Don Antonio.)

SCRIVANO. (*to Don Antonio*) You seem to be a little mistaken, Don Antonio; you think whole of the plantation is adjudged to you?

DON ANTONIO. To be sure. Don Felix himself admits that he has no right to it, and that he has opposed my petition only to gain time to get in his crops.

SCRIVANO. Then, Senor, you arc mistaken. The lands in dispute are given in equal shares between you. (*during thin discourse, the Judge walks about the stage shaking the money-bag*)

DON ANTONIO. Senor Bertoldo, is it possible that you have decreed one half of *my* plantation to Don Felix?

DON BERTOLDO. *Your* plantation? Correct your speech.

DON ANTONIO. Every one knows it is mine.

DON BERTOLDO. Then every one is mistaken; as they will soon learn from my irrevocable decree. I tell you, I have patiently examined all the writings, and carefully investigated every law that can apply in your case—neither did I forget, good Senor, to allow due force to certain weighty arguments with which you, as well as Don Felix, had furnished me.

DON ANTONIO. (*aside*) I see how it is, (*to the Judge*) Senor—(*gives him a purse*)—here is a purse, containing the last doubloon I possess in the world. I raised the money yesterday on the credit of the decree, which, it was generally thought, you would give in my favor.

DON BERTOLDO. Well, Senor, it is but right that you should consider yourself *debtor* to the decree, in the sum for which you obtained *credit* upon it. We'll re-consider the case. You may retire.

DON ANTONIO. (*aside*) And never, I trust, be compelled to seek justice from such a polluted tribunal!

[*Exit.*

DON BERTOLDO. (*counts the money*) Here is just another thousand dollars. Let Don Antonio then have two hundred acres more than I before intended. That is only at the rate of five dollars an acre, which is extremely cheap for such excellent land.

SCRIVANO. Don Antonio never made so good a purchase.——The next suit, Senor, that appears on my list, is that between Mr. George Wilkinson, one of the American settlers, and our countryman, Don Gusman de Passamontes, for a email farm, consisting of fifty acres of good cotton land, and as many of useless pine-barren.

DON BERTOLDO. What says the fee-book?

SCRIVANO. Not a word. Neither party has given a dollar.

DON BERTOLDO. Insolent knaves! How dare they trouble me with their quarrels? But I'll be even with them. I decree then that the cotton land be sold to pay the other officers of justice the expences of the suit, and that one half of the pine-barren be given to each of the parties.

SCRIVANO. Ha, ha, ha! That's the wisest and withal the merriest decision I ever heard.

DON BERTOLDO. You see I make no national distinctions—no difference between the American and the Spanish suitor. Forbid it, Justice, that ever such illiberality should be found in this tribunal!

SCRIVANO. Or any other distinction but what appears in the fee-book.

DON BERTOLDO. Right; for he who makes the richest present may be reasonably supposed to be the richest man; and he who has most riches in this country, we should consider as the most industrious. Now, as industry is the source of honesty and just dealing, we should *always* decide in favor of the most industrious—that is, of him whose honest exertions enable him to make us the richest present.

SCRIVANO. Most excellent reasoning, indeed!

Enter a SERVANT.

SERVANT. The Widow Sanchez requests admittance.

SCRIVANO. (*to the Judge*) This woman has no money—she will only tease your worship, if you admit her.

DON BERTOLDO. (*to the Servant*) Shew her in. [*Exit Servant.*] Her friends may have assisted her on this occasion.

Enter WIDOW SANCHEZ.

WIDOW SANCHEZ. I presume, Senor, to come into your presence to ask if the affairs of my deceased husband, now before your worship's tribunal, are yet settled?

DON BERTOLDO. I am engaged on other business, woman. Withdraw.

WIDOW SANCHEZ. Senor, I entreat you to recollect, that I have no other support for myself and my orphan children than the produce of that small farm of my husband's, which your worship has kept possession of so long.

DON BERTOLDO. How then have you existed these four years past? (*aside*) for I have had it all that time.

WIDOW SANCHEZ. By the bounty of my friends. I hope, Senor, you will have the goodness to restore me the land, and allow me some rent, be it ever so little.

DON BERTOLDO. I tell you, woman, you ought to be much obliged to me for taking care of it for you. Though indeed it is our duty to protect the property of the widow and the orphan.

WIDOW SANCHEZ. Was it requisite, Senor, to exhaust the soil, already poor enough, by taking from it four crops of tobacco?

DON BERTOLDO. To be sure, woman; to make it produce the better wheat for you. Withdraw, I say.

(The Scrivano speaks to her apart.)

WIDOW SANCHEZ. Well, Senor, if I make over one half of the farm to you, will your worship let me have the remainder.

DON BERTOLDO. (*with politeness*) By all means, Sonora; by all means. Indeed, I am well entitled to *one* half of the land, for improving and lightening so much the soil of the whole.

SCRIVANO. It shall be done, good lady, as his worship is pleased to direct. Retire.

WIDOW. It is not in my power, Senor, to make you a suitable return—(*aside*) but I trust the devil soon will.

[Exit.

DON BERTOLDO. Scrivano, you shall have half of my share of this farm.

SCRIVANO. May your worship live a thousand years.

Enter SERVANT.

SERVANT. Don Joseph, the watch-maker, requests admittance.

DON BERTOLDO. Let him come. [*Exit Servant.*] I suppose it is about that shed he calls a house, which he wants me to take from the right owner and give to him; but I wont though—unless he pays down half the worth of it at least.

Enter DON JOSEPH.

DON BERTOLDO. What do you want, sir?

DON JOSEPH. To sell your worship an elegant gold repeating watch.

DON BERTOLDO. To sell, sir?

DON JOSEPH. Yes, Senor, but very cheap. I can afford to let your worship have it for one dollar.

DON BERTOLDO. (*taking the watch*) Well, Don Joseph, on these terms we shall deal.

DON JOSEPH. Has it pleased your worship to make a decree concerning that small house?

DON BERTOLDO. Justice shall be done, my good friend; you may retire. [*Exit Don Joseph.*] Decree him the house, Scrivano.

Scrivano. Has the other party made any present, Senor?

Don Bertoldo. Not a maravedi.[26] The fool resolved to depend on what he called the justice of his cause.

Scrivano. Then all is right. I apprehended your worship might have forgotten.

Don Bertoldo. Never fear me.

Enter **Servant.**

Servant. Don Rodriguez, Senor.

Don Bertoldo. Let him come. (*Exit Servant.*) This is the troublesome old fellow that lay in jail three years on suspicion of doubting the authority of the Pope to grant pardons for murder, and ten years more for complaining of being kept so long in confinement without a trial. He comes, I suppose, to beg for his property.

Enter **Don Rodriguez.**

Don Rodriguez. Once more, Senor, let me beseech you to restore to me my property, which was sequestrated when I was first put in prison, thirteen years ago. Surely, as the slightest degree of guilt has not been fixed upon me, and that I have been, in consequence, liberated by the king's order, I hope you will not deem my request unreasonable.

Don Bertoldo. You want the whole of your property, I suppose?

Don Rodriguez. I certainly have a right to it.

Don Bertoldo. Unconscionable knave! To make no allowance for thirteen years' board and lodging.

---

26. A medieval Spanish coin.

SCRIVANO. Ha, ha, ha!—And for such *secure* apartments, and such luxurious diet—the best bread and water in the universe!

DON BERTOLDO. Begone, instantly! You are an abominable, wicked, seditious old man. I know you dislike our government—you are a traitor, sir, to your king.

DON RODRIGUEZ. No, Senor; they are the worst of traitors who render his authority odious, by abusing it to gratify their own avarice or malice. Would to heaven that he knew what sort of magistrates he employs on this side of the Atlantic. But better times are coming—He may be undeceived. At all events, the American government will do us justice!

[*Exit.*

DON BERTOLDO. (*in anger*) I'll send the villain to jail again.

SCRIVANO. You had better not, Senor. There are perhaps too many there already of the old standers. The Americans may abuse us.

DON BERTOLDO. For what? If these prisoners had money, they would not be where they are; and without money, what would they do any where else?

Enter **SERVANT.**

SERVANT. Mr. Fairtrade, Senor.

DON BERTOLDO. Let him come in. (*Exit Servant.*) Who is this?

SCRIVANO. The keen New-England smuggler, that took in the Dutch Jew[27] so cleverly.

---

27. A racist portrayal of a character who never appears onstage. Described as both shady and greedy, this depiction fits with the anti-Semitic sentiments, mostly inherited from Europe, which many European-Americans felt toward Jewish-Americans at this time.

DON BERTOLDO. How was that?

SCRIVANO. The Jew sold him a quantity of cotton at the full price, having first half filled the bales with sand to make them weigh the better. The New-England-man detected the cheat, and to be even with the Dutchman, paid him with rum-casks filled with salt water, except a bladder of rum fixed to the bung-hole of each. The Jew was in such a hurry to close the bargain, that he let Fairtrade set sail with the cotton, before he examined the rum.

Enter **FAIRTRADE.**

DON BERTOLDO. What's your business, sir?

FAIRTRADE. (*speaks with a nasal twang*) Please your honor, I've come up from my vessel that has just anchored below the fort, and I am going to a neighboring plantation in my boat, with a few onions and other small *notions*.

DON BERTOLDO. To smuggle, no doubt. Let the boat be immediately examined, Alguazils!

FAIRTRADE. Pray, your honor, stop for a little. Does your honor want any butter? I have brought a *pound or two* as a present to your honor.

DON BERTOLDO. Damn your butter, fellow—Let the boat be searched, I say. If I find a single contraband article in it, you shall be sent to amuse yourself seven years in chains on the public works.

FAIRTRADE. I'll add a small cheese to the butter.

DON BERTOLDO. Insolent rogue! Do you suppose such things would induce *me* to suffer the king's revenue to be defrauded? Smuggling, sir, is a most abominable offence—I cannot suffer it to pass unpunished.

FAIRTRADE. Please your honor, we'll put half a barrel of flour and a few bunches of onions to the cheese and butter.

DON BERTOLDO. Unparalleled assurance! The villain presumes to offer me a bribe. (*aside to Fairtrade*) A bribe of cheese and onions. Couldn't you add a little garlic to it, or some other such *notion*, mister? (*Don Bertoldo walks to the side of the stage.*)

SCRIVANO. Mr. Fairtrade, I am astonished that a man of your good sense and experience can behave yourself so foolishly. Don't you know that his honor never takes any thing but money? The flour and the other things you offered to *him*, are only suitable for *me*. Let your servant leave them at my house; but if you wish to escape seven years' slavery, you must find cash for his honor.

FAIRTRADE. (*aside*) What a confounded conscience some people have! but I suppose I can't help it. (*to Don Bertoldo*) Please your honor, the whole that I have in my boat is worth very little.

DON BERTOLDO. (*takes off his spectacles*) I tell you what, Mr. Fairtrade, if I happen to see your boat as she passes, I cannot, consistently with my sacred duty and my oaths of office, allow her to proceed unexamined. Now the method I adopt to reconcile my obliging disposition with my conscience is, to take the glasses out of my spectacles, and put in the place of them, something through which I cannot possibly see.

FAIRTRADE. A very good way, I vow. Here's a two-cent piece of copper; put it into your honor's spectacles, and I'll swear you won't be able to see through it.

DON BERTOLDO. Fool, do you think that *copper* can blind *me*? a mole could see through it.

FAIRTRADE. Well, mister, here's a dollar. That will do, I guess.

DON BERTOLDO. No, mister, it won't do. I have the eye of a lynx. All metals but gold are so porous, that I can see through them easily.

FAIRTRADE. (*aside*) I vow his honor is a very great knave. (*takes a small piece of gold out of his purse—a half-joe*[28]) Here, please your honor.

DON BERTOLDO. (*tries to put the half-joe into the spectacles*) This won't fit, Senor Smuggler. My spectacles will take the full size of a doubloon.

FAIRTRADE. (*aside*) I swear, I marvel that Satan suffers you to tarry on the earth. (*aloud*) Here, your honor—behold a doubloon! But don't forget to return me the half-joe.

DON BERTOLDO. (*takes the one and returns the other—places the doubloon in the spectacles and puts them on*) Now, good sir, *one* eye is completely covered, but 1 can see very well with the other eye still.

FAIRTRADE. (*aside*) Oh, nation to your maw of a conscience. The whale that swallowed Jonas[29] was not half so voracious—(*to Don Bertoldo*) Here, sir, take it. (*gives another doubloon*)

DON BERTOLDO. Very well, worthy sir; now I cannot see in the least, your boat may pass. Retire.

[*Fairtrade runs off.*

DON BERTOLDO. What makes the fellow scamper away so last?

SCRIVANO. Perhaps he has cheated your worship—see if the doubloons are good.

---

28. A small Portuguese coin.

29. According to the Old Testament (Jonah 2:1-11), a whale (or in the Hebrew Bible, a fish) swallowed the reluctant prophet Jonah, whom God had charged with preaching repentance to the city of Nineveh.

Don Bertoldo. (*sounds the doubloons*) Cased dollars,[30] by my integrity!—Holloa! Alguazils, stop that villain! Stop him! Run out and have him seized! (*Exit Scrivano*) Oh, the knave! the cheat!—To be taken in by such a rascal—

Enter **Scrivano.**

Scrivano. I have sent after the rogue; but I fear he cannot be taken—(*cannon heard—looks out at a window*)—Senor, the French Prefect is just taking possession of the fort. The colours of his nation are already displayed. Your worship's authority, I fear, is at an end.

Don Bertoldo. No matter. If I could catch this scoundrel, I'd send him off on board the frigate, at all hazards. To be insulted with base coin!—I could forgive any thing sooner. Damn the villain!—(*The saluting of cannon is heard.*)

A **Servant** *enters.*

Servant. We have not been able to overtake this man, Senor; he jumped into his boat and rowed off.

Don Bertoldo. It can't be helped. Come, Scrivano, collect my papers, and prepare to set sail with me. Oh, if I had that Yankee rascal by the ear, I'd teach him what it is to defraud an *upright* Spanish judge.

[*Exit.*

---

30. Meaning coins of a lesser value covered by a thin layer of higher-value metal to pass them off as real.

ACT V.
SCENE—A Library.

Enter PHELIM O'FLINN, LUCY MARGLAND, THERESA
and FATHER FRANCISCO—*Lucy is dressed as Laura, and veiled.*

FATHER FRANCISCO. Now, my children, your marriage is complete;
and nothing but the death of one of you can dissolve it. I go to
record it in a public manner, lest any objection should hereafter
arise, or either of you be ever base enough to deny or attempt
to invalidate it.

[*Exit.*

PHELIM. What could put it into his reverence's noddle that either of
us would ever dream of denying our marriage? If no one else dis-
turb us, no fear of our bothering ourselves. And now, my jewel,
sure you wont be after making any more objections against my
kissing you. Turn up that muslin petticoat you have got on your
head, and let myself have a peep at your sweet face once more.

LUCY. (*aside to Theresa*) I dread his seeing me, till the affair is explained to him.

THERESA. (*to her*) Leave that to me, and I'll do it bye and bye. (*to
Phelim*) Captain, this dear timid young lady is so flustrated,
(and no wonder—I should be so myself) that she is afraid of
fainting. You must let me take her to her own chamber till she
recovers her spirits.

PHELIM. Well I'll consint, my dear, (*to Lucy*) if you promise to let
me pay you a visit in that same chamber, as soon as you have
got the better of the frustration.

THERESA. She agrees; but she's not able to speak, poor clear lady. I am sure if I was in her situation, my heart would be so full of what was before me, that I could not get a word out.

[*Exit Theresa and Lucy.*

PHELIM. But I'll be bound you could leer consint, at least, my gay ould dowager.

Enter SENORA DE LA PLATA

SENORA DE LA PLATA. So, sir, I learn that your marriage has been already solemnized. You might have had the good-manners, if not the gratitude, to have informed me of it.

PHELIM. I wanted to do so, my dear, but Senora Laura herself prevented me.

Enter DON BERTOLDO

DON BERTOLDO. Where's Laura? Every thing is ready for our departure, (*seeing Phelim*) Ha! Who is this?

SENORA DE LA PLATA. Laura, my love, is married to this gentleman.

DON BERTOLDO. Nonsense! Where's Laura, I say? She must come with me directly.

PHELIM. (*aside*) Oh, this is the ould villain of a judge, her, guardian—(*aloud*) No, my dear, this night, if you please, Mrs. Laura shall set sail with me, on our first matrimonial voyage, for the land of delight.

DON BERTOLDO. Are *you* mad too? Who *are* you, sir?

SENORA DE LA PLATA. Laura's husband—havn't I told you.

PHELIM. (*aside*) Since all's safe, I may let it out. (*aloud*) Yes; I am Laura's husband.

DON BERTOLDO. Villain! 'tis false.

PHELIM. Have a care, honey; or you'll get the best beating ever you had in your life.

DON BERTOLDO. I ask you, who *are* you? What's your name?

PHELIM. Phelan O'Flinn, *Esquire*, that never yet was afraid or ashamed of any tiling—and so take care of yourself, my ould lad; for if you are after attempting to take Mrs. Laura or her dollars away from me, you may count yourself as well-leathered a man as any in America.

SENORA DE LA PLATA. (*calmly*) Bless me, sir, I thought you were Captain O'Brien!

DON BERTOLDO. Distraction! Explain this to me, madam, instantly.

SENORA DE LA PLATA. I will, my soul's idol; but don't be in such a fury. This man having heard, I suppose, that Laura had a fortune, and loved Captain O'Brien, has personated that gentleman, imposed upon both her and me, and prevailed on my dear child to marry him immediately. Father Francisco has just performed the ceremony.

DON BERTOLDO. Damnation! What do I hear!

SENORA DE LA PLATA. Indeed I am very sorry for *her*, and for *you* also, my love.

DON BERTOLDO. Hell and confusion! I see how it is. This is your work, madam. But your machinations shall not yet deprive me of Laura. This villain shall be taken in irons to the Havana, and imprisoned in one of the dungeons of the Moro[31] till the executioner sets him free. Laura shall yet go with me to Spain; and as for you, madam, I shall leave you to the detestation you deserve.

---

31. A misspelling of Morro Castle, the fortress that guarded Havana port in Cuba.

PHELIM. (*astonished*) What's all this?

SENORA DE LA PLATA. Thank you, my darling—Take Laura with you by all means, and this fellow also. But don't mistake and carry away Captain O'Brien in his stead, my soul's idol.

[*Exit, laughing.*

DON BERTOLDO. Ho, there! Scrivano! Alguazhs!

PHELIM. I say, honey, what are you going to be after doing?

Enter SCRIVANO *and* ALGUAZILS.

DON BERTOLDO. (*to one of the Alguazils*) Bring handcuffs and fetters to put on this scoundrel, that he may be sent prisoner on board the frigate directly. He is an impostor, a robber, a murderer, an heretic!

AN ALGUAZILS. An heretic! Then, by Saint Anthony,[32] I'll get the heaviest irons I can find for him.

[*Exit Alguazil.*

DON BERTOLDO. (*apart to Scrivano*) Do you remain here with these alguazils to guard the miscreant, while I go to secure Laura and prepare for our departure.

[*Exit Don Bertoldo.*

PHELIM. Blood and ouns, what are you all about?

SCRIVANO. (*calmly*) Only preparing to punish you as your guilt deserves.

PHELIM. Now be aisy, my dear. Is it joking you are? Sure you wouldn't be after punishing any one without giving him a fair trial?

32. St. Anthony was an important theologian and teacher of the Franciscan order in the Catholic Church who was said to have performed many miracles.

SCRIVANO. By no means. You shall have the fairest trial imaginable. Our proceedings, though rather slow, are *very sure* at last. In the first place, we shall take whatever property we can find belonging to you, as property would be only an incumbrance to a man confined in a dungeon, and allowed no other nourishment but bread and water.

PHELIM. Oh, sweet bad luck to you!

SCRIVANO. Then when you've lain there long enough to become *quite cool,* and to recollect yourself perfectly, which may not, perhaps, require more than two or three years, your first examination will take place.

PHELIM. Examination! What will they examine me for?

SCRIVANO. To learn whether you are guilty or not; as no one can know this so well as yourself.

PHELIM. But where, my dear, would be the use of asking *me* such questions? Do they think a body would be such a fool as to tell them the *truth?*

SCRIVANO. If you do confess the truth, your sufferings will be short— The halter or the wheel will put you out of pain in a twinkling.

PHELIM. Oh, murder! Is it come to this at last! Sure enough, Father Farrel often told me I wasn't born to be drowned.

SCRIVANO. If you do not tell the truth, but obstinately persist that you are innocent—

PHELIM. What will they do to me then?

SCRIVANO. Why then, should you have the good fortune to be tried by a *merciful* judge, he will order your flesh to be only *slightly* pinched with a pair of tongs not *quite* red hot—or your thumbs to be squeezed in a very *agreeable* little screw—or the soles of your feet to get a *gentle* toasting before a *slow* fire.

Enter the **ALGUAZIL.** *with handcuffs, &c.—also* **SAWNY.**

PHELIM. (*to Sawny*) Sawny, my dear, are you there? I'm glad to see you. I'm in great trouble.

SAWNY. I was afraid that a' was na right wi ye; and it was that made me insist on coming to see ye.

PHELIM. Good luck to you, my dear. (*they converse apart*)

SCRIVANO. (*to the Alguazil who last entered*) Who is this other fellow?

ALGUAZIL. An accomplice of the heretic's, I suppose. He came here in spite of me.

SCRIVANO. Fetch another pair of handcuffs for *him*.

[*Exit Alguazil.*

(*Sawny and Phelim come forward and converse apart.*)

SAWNY. Gude troth, it's an unlucky business.

PHELIM Oh, Sawny, my dear, this is the way I'm always taken in, whenever I lay a good scheme to earn an honest bit of bread, and lay up something for the rest of my life. I'm sure to fail at last, though I *mean* every thing so well. Isn't it cruel now of these thieves to rob me both of my wife and my fortune?

SAWNY. If they were to tak only the *wife*, and leave the *siller*, I'd think nathing at a' aboot it. My ten thousand dollars a' gone.

PHELIM. (*apart to Sawny*) Blood and ouns, sweet Sawny, will we be after letting these blackguards get the better of us? Sure there's only nine or ten of them; and there's as nate a proker and pair of tongs as a man need desire. If we could make our escape from these tormentors, and get to New-Orleans, we might still secure the wife and the cash. Sure you wont refuse to lend me a hand now that I have a good cause to fight for.

SAWNY. The cause is a vary gude one, for there's siller to be gained in it. I'd hae nathing to do wi' a bad cause, for I'm vary honest.

PHELIM. Long life to you, my honest fellow.

Enter DON BERTOLDO.

DON BERTOLDO. All is now ready—Come along.

PHELIM. Wait a bit, my dear, if you please. (*goes to the fire-place, takes a poker, and gives a pair of tongs to Sawny*) Take hould of this, honey, and play away like a true-born Scot. Ould *Ireland* and Scotland for ever!

SAWNY. Auld *Scotland* and Ireland for ever! (*they attack the judge and his party*)

DON BERTOLDO. Villains! Ruffians!—What do you mean! Help! Murder!

PHELIM. (*pursuing and beating the judge*) Well done, Sawny. Ogh, how it delights my own heart to have the leathering of a limb of the law.

DON BERTOLDO. Help—Murder—Mercy!

PHELIM. Aye, aye, my lad—You shall have the same mercy you shew to others yourself. You'd pinch my flesh—screw my thumbs—toast my feet—Eh? How do you like this? Well, by my soul, I'd never desire a better bit of shilelah nor a good iron proker. (*drives Don Bertoldo and Alguazils off the stage.*) Huzza! the day is our own! Give us your hand, honest Sawny.

Voices without. Bring fire-arms—get the blunderbuss—assemble all the servants.

PHELIM. Keep fast the door, Sawny! What must we do now? By the powers, if it wasn't for their shooting irons, myself wouldn't value them a rap. Wait—Let me hould a bit of a caucus with myself. (*pauses*)

Without. Burst the door—Shoot the ruffians.

PHELIM. (*goes to the window*) I see one of the American regiments just marching into the city. Oh, to be sure, there isn't my sweet little eagle, just ready to take us under his wings, and caress us with his talents.

(*Attempt made to burst open the doer.*)

DON BERTOLDO. (*without*) Fire at them through the door!

SAWNY. Phelim, d'ye hear? We had better gang oot at the window, and mak the best of oor way to the city,

PHELIM. Right, laddie, and I'll get a party of these brave American boys to come back with me and rescue my sweet wife.

SAWNY. And her *dollars* too, Phelim.

PHELIM. Oh, when I spake of the one, my dear, I always mean the other. (*they go to the window*) Wait, Sawny—We must leave the tongs and the proker behind us. If we were to take them away, these thieves might call it *stealing*, and put us to trouble.

SAWNY. I'm glad ye are so cautious, Phelim.

[*Exit at the window.*

The Judge and his party force open the door and enter.

DON BERTOLDO. Where are the villains?

SCRIVANO. Gone out at the window, I suppose. (*going towards the window*) Aye, there they are, making the best of their way towards the city.

DON BERTOLDO. Pursue them—seize them—shoot them.

SCRIVANO. If I might take the liberty to advise, it would be better to leave them, and get Laura away immediately. My lady has assured me that your ward has been lawfully married to the impostor; so that he may, perhaps, claim not only herself but her fortune from your worship.

Don Bertoldo. It may be so. Let's begone then instantly. Confound the ruffian, how he has made my bones ache.

[*Exeunt.*

SCENE—another apartment.

Senora de la Plata. (*reading a letter*) Captain O'Brien's compliments—requests permission to do himself the honor of paying his respects. Hum—all's well—O'Brien here, and Laura going to the Havanna—I must detain him, however, till she is *actually* on board—Perhaps if she were to see him, she might refuse to go.

Enter **Servant.**

Servant. Captain O'Brien, Senora.

Senora de la Plata. Shew him up instantly. (*exit Servant*) Now to improve the impression I have already made.

Enter **Captain O'Brien.**

Captain O'Brien. Allow me, madam, to have the honor of paying you my profound respects. I have thought it an age since I last had the felicity of your charming conversation.

Senora de la Plata. Captain O'Brien is welcome to Louisiana.

Captain O'Brien. I need hardly enquire, madam, if you are well. Your animated countenance, and the lustre of those eyes, sufficiently indicate your health, as well as the bright intelligence of your accomplished mind. (*aside*) I suppose I shall be taxed with an hour of this flattery before I can get a sight of Laura. But as no other means will obtain it, I must submit.

SENORA DE LA PLATA. What, sir, have you studied flattery in the wilderness?

CAPTAIN O'BRIEN. Oh, no, madam; I am ignorant of what it is. My soul is simplicity itself—alive, indeed, to the impressions of beauty, genius and taste; while my tongue expresses, without consideration, the sentiments of my heart. But I am fearful I offend. The modest diffidence, which is ever the companion of such exalted perfections as *your's*, would suspect the severest truth for the language of adulation.

SENORA DE LA PLATA. Tasteful youth. (*aside*)

CAPTAIN O'BRIEN. (*aside*) After that, I think I may venture to ask for Laura. (*aloud*) I hope Donna Laura has been well, madam, since I had the honor of seeing her with you?

SENORA DE LA PLATA. No, sir. (*laconically*)

CAPTAIN O'BRIEN. Is she at home, madam?

SENORA DE LA PLATA. No, sir.

CAPTAIN O'BRIEN. In the city, perhaps?

SENORA DE LA PLATA. No, sir.

CAPTAIN O'BRIEN. Not indisposed I hope, for your sake, as you love her so well.

SENORA DE LA PLATA. Somewhat indisposed, I believe, and gone to take the air—(*aside*) where, I hope, you'll never see her.

CAPTAIN O'BRIEN. (*aside*) It wont do yet. I've begun too soon. (*aloud*) She is very young, madam, I believe.

SENORA DE LA PLATA. A mere child—yet there are those who admire such babies.

CAPTAIN O'BRIEN. Mine is a very different taste. I admire the rich and mellowed charms of maturity. The charms of that heavenly person, whose intelligence adds lustre, and whose taste and talents give an indescribable fascination to her beauty.

SENORA DE LA PLATA. (*aside*) Elegant creature.

CAPTAIN O'BRIEN. Yes, madam, when beauty like your's is arrayed in the robe of Minerva,[33] and clasped by the zone of the graces, the love which it inspires, like the rapture afforded by a celestial visitation, is almost too much for mortals to bear.

SENORA DE LA PLATA. Beauty without intelligence is like the statue of Pygmalion[34] before it felt the divine spark—There, sir, (*pointing to a picture*) is an attempt of my feeble pencil to represent that story.

CAPTAIN O'BRIEN. Admirable! What expression! How divinely are *all* the muscles delineated!

SENORA DE LA PLATA. And what think you of this Daphne and Apollo?[35]

CAPTAIN O'BRIEN. Wonderful! The lightness and transparency of the nymph's drapery make the piece exquisitely interesting. Please to favor me, madam, with some of your new poetical productions? Have you finished the elegy you were composing on the death of your little female dog, Louise, that was drowned in attempting to swim across the river to visit the dear object of her affections.

---

33. From Roman mythology, Minerva is the goddess of wisdom as well as handcrafts.

34. From Greek mythology, Pygmalion was the king of Cyprus who carved a female statue of ivory, after which Aphrodite (goddess of beauty, sexual love, and fertility) gave the figure life.

35. From Greco-Roman mythology, Daphne was a nymph, a nature spirit, who, in order to escape her pursuer Apollo, god of music, poetry, and medicine, was transformed into a laurel tree.

Senora de la Plata. No, sir; I have attempted another subject—but I'm afraid you'll think it rather too mean for the dignity of the muse.

Captain O'Brien. Impossible! *Your* talents, madam, could elevate the meanest subject.

Senora de la Plata. The trifle of which I speak is a supposed poetical epistle from a musquito in New-Orleans, to her love in the country; inviting him to repair to town, and partake of the fresh and delicious repasts which the continual influx of strangers promises to afford abundantly for the remainder of the year.

Captain O'Brien. A thought worthy of the imagination of Shakspeare. In what glowing colours will the poetical insect describe the personal characteristics of the countries whose natives are about to visit Louisiana. How luxuriantly will she expatiate on the various beauties which are to afford her race so much amusement as well as food.

Senora de la Plata. I find that your taste in poetry, as well as in painting, is excellent.

Captain O'Brien. But I beg pardon for so long neglecting to enquire for Don Bertoldo. I hope he intends to remain with his family in this province.

Senora de la Plata. Ah, sir, he has determined on returning to Spain.

Captain O'Brien. It is cruel in him thus to rob the society of New-Orleans of its brightest ornament.

Senora de la Plata. And what is worse, he intends to leave me behind him. The very idea of it overcomes me. Nay, he is in hopes of obtaining a divorce from me through his own misconduct. Indeed he has treated me with great——But he is yet my husband, and it becomes me to suffer in silent resignation.

CAPTAIN O'BRIEN. Incomparable lady! Patient yet lovely in grief!

SENORA DE LA PLATA. If he does succeed in obtaining the divorce, I am sure I shall never marry again.

CAPTAIN O'BRIEN. Ah! madam, do not resolve too hastily.

SENORA DE LA PLATA. Never—never. I shall never marry again.

CAPTAIN O'BRIEN. Consider further, madam. Present to your amiable mind the faithful and soothing picture of a fortunate union. Imagine the lovely bride, folded in the arms, and pressed to the heart of a tender, ardent, adoring husband, whose tongue utters the soft yet thrilling accents, while his eyes dart forth the electric fire of love!—A happy wife—a delighted mother!

SENORA DE LA PLATA. Sir—sir! I (*musket shot heard from without*)

Enter THERESA.

THERESA. Where's Captain O'Brien?

CAPTAIN O'BRIEN. I am he—What's the matter?

THERESA. Oh, sir, come and protect your Laura. Don Bertoldo and his Alguazils are now endeavoring to carry her off by force. They have been attacked by two men who came here this morning from the Natchez, and who, on hearing her cries, ran to her assistance. (*O'Brien is running out.*)

SENORA DE LA PLATA. Stay, Captain, stay—Laura is married to one of those men.

CAPTAIN O'BRIEN Married!

THERESA. No, Captain, she is *not* married—nor will she marry any one but you, if you deserve her. Don't believe Senora de la Plata—she has done every thing in her power to ruin Donna Laura. Come along, and I'll tell you the whole. Oh, you wicked lady! 'Twould be unpardonable even in an unmarried young woman like me, to set my cap at a gentleman already engaged.

[*Exeunt O'Brien and Theresa.*

SENORA DE LA PLATA. Stay—I charge you, stay. What! am I disobeyed, neglected, scorned and abandoned?—Have I been the dupe of this traitor's passion for Laura?—Monstrous! horrible!—Let the torch of love become the fire-brand of a fury. What shall I do first?—Pursue and tear them both to pieces. No; I'll send assistance to Don Bertoldo, to enable him to carry Laura away.

[*Exit.*

*SCENE—A Public Place or Square in New-Orleans—
view of the fort, with the French flag displayed—
troops marching—the American general and his suite—
the French prefect—citizens, soldiers, &c.*

FRENCH PREFECT. Now, general, I deliver to you possession of the province.

GENERAL. (*to an aid-de-camp*) Let the American colours be then hoisted on the fort.

(*The French colours are gradually lowered half way down the flag-
staff, and those of the United States hoisted up to them.
They remain together for a short time. The latter are then
hoisted to top, and the former lowered down entirely.
Martial music, saluting of cannon, &c.*

Enter **CAPTAIN O'BRIEN, PHELIM** and **SAWNY**, dragging in
DON BERTOLDO, SCRIVANO and **ALGUAZILS.**

GENERAL. What occasions this disturbance?

CAPTAIN O'BRIEN. I regret, general, that the rights of injured innocence compel me to interrupt the joy and harmony which on this happy occasion should universally prevail. I bring before you the judge, Don Bertoldo de la Plata, who has attempted, for the most flagitious purposes, to carry away by force from this province his ward, the young and lovely Laura de Villaverde; but, with the assistance of these, two brave men, I have defeated his foul project. I claim then for her the protection of your authority, and I trust you will deal with this perfidious villain as his guilt deserves.

PHELIM. And, please your honor, 1 claim the sweet cratur for myself—and, by my soul, no one has so good a right to her for all their fine spaking, because myself is the young lady's husband.

GENERAL. What say you, Senor, to this accusation?

DON BERTOLDO. Can your excellency ask me such a question? Do you not know that I am a person of the first rank in the province? That alone is a sufficient answer to the calumny of those wretches.

GENERAL. Not so, Senor—LIBERTY IS NOW IN LOUISIANA!—The government which now rules here will not admit your rank as the testimony of your innocence; nor suffer it to shelter you if you have acted wrong. Our laws confer no privilege which justice may refuse to recognise—the humblest are shielded by their protection—the proudest oppressor is not beyond the reach of their avenging power.

DON BERTOLDO. What means all this jargon? I tell you I insist on having these scoundrels hanged up immediately, for daring to insult Don Bertoldo de la Plata.

GENERAL. I cannot comply with your desire, Senor. No man within the pale of our authority can suffer an ignominious death, until a fair and public trial by those *whose own interest is justice* shall have indubitably ascertained his guilt. Life would be of mean estimation indeed if held as you would wish—but at a tyrant's mercy.

PHELIM. Well said, your honor, by my soul!

SAWNY. Haud your tongue, Phelim—Dunna mak sae free wi your betters.

DON BERTOLDO. Don't you know, General, that I am a judge? Do you suppose that I don't know what the law is?

GENERAL. Though not perhaps, Senor, what it ought to be.

DON BERTOLDO. Well, if your excellency cannot hang the villains off at once, I hope you wont make any ceremony about fining them smartly for their impertinence, or laying them in jail till they learn to respect their superiors.

GENERAL. All such despotic proceedings as these, Senor, are inconsistent with the nature, and abhorrent to the spirit of our free constitution. Of what value would be the fruit of honest labour, if exposed, as you would have it, to the grasp of privileged rapine? Or what the personal freedom which Providence intends for man, if by such an arbitrary mandate as you solicit he could be laid in bonds?

PHELIM. That's right, General. Sind the ould thief himself to jail, and that will be better still. By my soul, Sawny, if all law was like this I'd never fall out with it.

SAWNY. Tul it fell oot wi you, Phelim.

GENERAL. You are accused, Senor, of violating the rights of one whom it is my duty to protect—I therefore again request to know what you have to say in your defence?

DON BERTOLDO. Well, since I must so far condescend, I assert, that my ward and I are the injured persons, and these miscreants the atrocious offenders. This ruffian before you, called Flinn, has found means to inveigle her into a marriage, and your unworthy officer, O'Brien, to share in the plunder of her fortune, has become his accomplice. The better to effect their vile purposes of dishonoring and robbing her, they have twice attempted to assassinate me, while endeavoring as a faithful guardian to rescue her from them, and place her, by the aid of your authority, beyond the reach of their infamous schemes.

SCRIVANO. I can swear very positively that I overheard Flinn and the Captain as they conversed together, about dividing Donna Laura's fortune between them, and throwing his worship into the river, that they might enjoy their plunder in security.

AN ALGUAZIL. I can swear to the truth of every word his worship and the Scrivano have said.

ANOTHER ALGUAZIL. And I can swear to all that, and a great deal more besides.

PHELIM. And, by the powers, I can swear as hard as the best of you all, you blackguards, that you all lie; and that there isn't one word of truth in all you have said, or all you will say about the matter.

SAWNY. (*aside to Phelim*) And whatever you swear, Phelim, I'll *say* it's true; but I winna tak my oath to it; for that might cost a mon his ears, and destroy his credit with the merchants.
GENERAL. Where is the young lady herself?

CAPTAIN O'BRIEN. She had not sufficiently recovered from her alarm to come with us; but she will be here presently, accompanied by those who will prove that both Don Bertoldo and Mr. Flinn are mistaken, and that the person and fortune of Donna Laura are still disengaged, and at her own free disposal.

PHELIM. (*to O'Brien*) Be aisy now, countryman—I was a little before hand with you, my dear—but don't grieve about that; for, by my soul, I've cut out cleverer follows than ever your father's son will make. Ah! here comes the jolly priest and the gay ould house-keeper. They'll soon set every thing to rights. (*aside to Sawny*) Mind now, Sawny, how foolish the Captain will look when he knows all. Och! by the powers, honest Phelim is too cute for the best of them.

Enter FATHER FRANCISCO, THERESA, LAURA *and* LUCY MARGLAND—
Laura and Lucy are dressed alike, and are both veiled.

PHELIM. (*observing Laura and Lucy*) Blood-and-ouns! am I married double? Myself has no objection to as many sweet-hearts as you please; but one wife at a time is quite sufficient.

FATHER FRANCISCO. (*leading Lucy towards Phelim*) This, sir, is the only lady you can claim as your wife. Please to remove your veil, madam.

[*Lucy unveils.*

(*At sight of her Phelim starts—Don Bertoldo expresses surprise—
Lucy stretches forth her arms the attitude of supplication.*)

PHELIM. Ogh, by the powers, I'm kilt!—(*to the priest*) Oh, you scandalous desaiver!—(*to Lucy*) Devil take you, Lucy, my dear, how could you have the conscience to seduce me this way.

GENERAL. (*to the priest*) Be so good, sir, to explain this extraordinary business.

FATHER FRANCISCO. Most willingly. I was informed a few hours ago by this good gentlewoman, Donna Theresa, that Mr. Flinn, assuming the name and character of Captain O'Brien, had come to Don Bertoldo's house, and solicited his ward in marriage; and that there had also arrived there a short time afterwards this young woman, to whom Flinn had been guilty of an injury, for which nothing but marriage could atone. It was proposed to me. and I considered it allowable, that the imposture he was attempting should be made the means of reparation to the person he had wrong'd; to effect which purpose, Lucy Margland, being veiled and dressed like Donna Laura, was by me lawfully married to him.

DON BERTOLDO. You served him right. I rejoice that my ward has escaped. And now, (*to the general*) I hope your excellency will direct that she be immediately restored to me.

Laura. I entreat your excellency will not do as Don Bertoldo desires. He is the most perfidious of guardians.

Theresa. Indeed he is, please your worship. The wicked dotard has taken it into his foolish old head to fall in love with Donna Laura, and all he wants is to keep her to himself, and prevent her from marrying this handsome young officer, whom she loves as heartily—(Nay, *we* need not blush at being in love, my dear)—as I do Mr. Sawny M'Gregor.

General. The young lady is perfectly competent to choose a protector for herself.

[Laura gives her hand to O'Brien.

Don Bertoldo. Perdition seize you all together. I wish every American in the world broil'd on St. Anthony's gridiron.

[Exeunt Bertoldo, the Scrivano and Alguazils.

Phelim. Instead of the hundred thousand dollars I expected, nothing but the bad sixpence returned on my hands.

Captain O'Brien. Come, sir. be of good cheer. To your courage the safety of this lady is in a great measure due. It is her intention to make you a generous recompence, provided you are kind to Lucy Margland.

Phelim.. (*considers for a moment, and then to have determined; aside*) Phelim will be a squire at last—(*aloud*) Lucy O'Flinn, my dear, if you please. May be you think I did not know who she was all this time. Sure I only pritended I didn't, just to humour the joke.

Sawny. That's right, Phelim, make the best o' your bargain.

Phelim. And now, Sawny, I'm thinking that roguery, after all, is a troublesome, disagreeable, unprofitable business. I never yet could gain much by it; though, by my soul, that wasn't for want of giving it a *very fair trial.* I believe we had better leave off our tricks, and turn honest in downright earnest.

SAWNY. I am always honest, Phelim; vary honest. I ha made love to this bonny lassie like an *honest mon*, Phelim; and we ha agreed to buckle too. Gude sooth, she's vary warm—a fine hoose and a muckle bag of doubloons will soon be between us baith.

CAPTAIN O'BRIEN. Then all's well at last, and every thing contributes to render more delightful to us the peaceful and mutually advantageous union which our country has had the happiness of effecting with this important and fortunate PROVINCE.

GENERAL. From the short scene that has now passed before you, my friends and fellow-citizens, you may learn to rejoice at the event by which, without a struggle or an effort, you become at once entitled to participate in all those privileges which the civilized and intelligent nations of the world consider inestimable, and which it has cost our ancestors many severe conflicts to acquire and preserve. In the attainment of your rights, no kindred blood of your's has been shed; no foreign army has desolated your land; no domestic dissentions have embittered your social intercourse, or disturbed your repose. Do you ask, what is this FREEDOM for which we deem no exertions too painful, no sacrifice too great? It is that possession which makes all others valuable. It is that *security against oppressions* which gives animation to the industry, energy to the enterprise, vigor to the intellect, and worth and dignity to the moral character of man. It augments our pleasures in prosperity, and affords us in misfortune the consolation of a rich and perennial spring of hope. You may appreciate more justly its exalted value by contemplating its reverse—*despotic rule*; that accursed system which palsies all the powers of the body and the mind; mars the beneficence of nature; defeats the bounteous purposes of God, and dries up or poisons all the fountains of felicity, rendering men miserable and abject, even in the intervals when it forbears to oppress, by the degrading fears and terrors which it continues to inspire. The LIBERTY we cherish consists in the laws which secure to us the enjoyment of all our natural and justly acquired advantages, and in the guarantees provided by our government for the preservation and improvement of those laws as well as for their equitable administration—*Legislative power delegated by those whom the laws are to protect—Trial by those whose own interest justice.*

We do not bring you a system of mere speculative excellence, but one which for centuries has been tried and approved. The TEMPLE we have reared to FREEDOM is founded on the *wisdom and experience of ancient and modern ages.* In its structure, *Gothic strength and Grecian beauty* are combined; and it is formed on a plan so wide and capacious, that all the members of the most extensive and diversified empire may find protection beneath its ample dome. The confederated states of which our commonwealth consists, compose an IMPERIAL GOVERNMENT, sufficiently united for national defence and those objects for which union and uniformity are requisite; and MUNICIPAL GOVERNMENTS sufficiently numerous, powerful and divided to adapt regulations suitable to the circumstances of each state; to augment our securities against usurpation, and to diffuse more widely these gratifying sentiments of confidence, independence and honest pride, which result from the right of managing our own important concerns. Do you require further proof or illustration of the excellence of *regulated freedom?* Look round you, and see in its effects its unequivocal panegyric. While TYRANNY, blasting and destroying every thing within the reach of its baleful influence, spreads desolation over cultivated plains, converts splendid cities into heaps of ruins, and reduces populous and once powerful nations to the abased condition of subject provinces, an easy prey to any enterprising foe—LIBERTY, like the forming power of Omnipotence, covers the barren heath with the cheerful abodes of men, crowns the bleakest mountains with the verdure of fertility, exalts feeble colonies into mighty commonwealths, and enables states of the most limited resources to resist, to confound, to overwhelm the proudest confederacies of unprincipled ambition. Cast your eyes on the country to which your's will be united—Observe her rapidly increasing population; her extended commerce; her teeming affluence; her advancement in all the useful and adorning arts of life; in a word, her universal prosperity, which neither the scourge of war nor the ravages of pestilence could arrest—in these you have the best commentary of her government and her laws. Henceforth, then, and for ever be your's all the privileges which constitute her freedom, her greatness and her glory—your's the just liberty of the press; the potent and ever-watchful guardian of a nation's rights; the sacred lamp of truth, that illuminates the world with an heavenly radiance—your's the incomparable trial by jury; the brightest gem in the diadem of a SOVEREIGN PEOPLE—your's, in a word, every barrier and safeguard we have erected to shield us from oppression.

FINALE,
TO BE SUNG BY THE AMERICAN CHARACTERS.

'Tis not the lust of sway or gold,
 That to our country your's unites;
In us, your faithful friends, behold
 The guardians of your sacred rights.

CHORUS.
For while upon yon tower, our banners wave,
Your land no tyrant ever shall enslave.

Oh, never may your people bear
 Of tyranny the galling chain,
Nor anarchy her scourges o'er them rear;
 But freedom with you ever reign.

For what avail the gifts of heav'n,
 The wealth which art from nature draws,
The affluence by commerce giv'n,
 Unless secured by Freedom's laws?

Hail Liberty, celestial maid,
 Columbia's glory and delight!
Here be thy brightest charms display'd,
 And all Columbia's sons UNITE.

For while upon yon tower, her banners wave,
This land no tyrant ever shall enslave.

THE END.

THE Music for the songs in this piece has been selected
by Mr. HODCKINSON, as follows:—
For the duet in page 9—*Bow, wow, wow.*
For the Song in pages 29 and 30—*Martough Delaney,*
Ditto in page 36—*The merry dance I dearly love.*
Ditto in page 44—*Charley over the water.*
For the finale in pages 102 and 103—*Return to Order,* in
the "Surrender of Teuton" from which the author has taken the
first line of the chorus, and the greatest part of the second verse
of the finale.

THE following are the principal passages
omitted in the representation:—

The whole of the 6th and the greater part of the 7th page.

Twenty-one lines from the top of page 15.

The greater part of page 17.

Part of the speech, and the whole of the song of Don
Bertoldo, in pages 18 and 19.

The last speech but one of Theresa's, in page 28.

The last two lines of page 34.

Theresa's songs in pages 36 and 44.

The last twenty lines of page 62.

The entire scene between Father Francisco and Phelim, at
the beginning of the 4th act.

The greater part of page 91.

And the parts of Don Antonio, Widow Sanchez and Don
Joseph in the scene of the Hall of Audience.